About the Author

Kerri was born and raised in the quaint city of East Providence, Rhode Island, and now resides in the bustling Northern Virginia area along with her husband and four beautiful children. Her journey from the tiny state of Rhode Island to Virginia wasn't just a geographical shift, but an exploration of life's myriad experiences and emotions that would later serve as the foundation of her powerful narratives. Kerri's writing is inspired by her personal experiences – her life's journey and her role as a mother of four. Kerri's book about stepmomming is more than just a story; it's a movement. She is committed to creating spaces where women's voices can be heard. Her hope is that this book will not only entertain and educate but will also empower women to express themselves freely and advocate for their rights. She is sparking a conversation, challenging societal norms, and opening doors for a new generation of women. Her words resonate with authenticity and courage, making her a voice to be reckoned with in today's literary world.

Stepmomming

Kerri Francis Bradley

Stepmomming

Olympia Publishers
London

www.olympiapublishers.com
OLYMPIA PAPERBACK EDITION

Copyright © Kerri Francis Bradley 2024

The right of Kerri Francis Bradley to be identified as author of
this work has been asserted in accordance with sections 77 and 78 of
the Copyright, Designs and Patents Act 1988.

All Rights Reserved

No reproduction, copy or transmission of this publication
may be made without written permission.
No paragraph of this publication may be reproduced,
copied or transmitted save with the written permission of the publisher,
or in accordance with the provisions
of the Copyright Act 1956 (as amended).

Any person who commits any unauthorized act in relation to
this publication may be liable to criminal
prosecution and civil claims for damage.

A CIP catalogue record for this title is
available from the British Library.

ISBN: 978-1-80439-130-3

First Published in 2024

Olympia Publishers
Tallis House
2 Tallis Street
London
EC4Y 0AB

Printed in Great Britain

Dedication

I dedicate this book to my partner and husband, Justin. Justin, you are the type of man all others aspire to be. Our journey as parents has not been without a few bumps, yet you have always been my teammate.

Introduction

I don't know who needs to hear this… actually, I know exactly who needs to hear this. Every stepmom out there in this very moment and every critic who thinks she is "out of her place," "overstepping," "not a real mom," or "isn't doing enough." Stepmomming is HARD AF. It doesn't matter who you are or how much you care, in fact, caring too much could be your problem. Not caring enough, could also be your problem. For every good and loving stepmom out there, there is a biological mom – a.k.a. bio mom – hating on her for it. Okay, maybe "every" is a slight exaggeration. I have met at least a handful of bio and stepmoms who get along decently well for their situations or at the very least respect one another or ignore one another enough to co-exist. Unfortunately, I have met even more stepmoms who suffer from an unforgiving, out-of-her-mind bio mom. In the stepmom community, we have all heard the stories of the bio moms who do not want their children's stepmothers around the children. Or the bio moms who prioritize men and drama over their children. There are whole stepmom support groups dedicated to bio mom trauma. Nevertheless, this book is not meant to demean bio moms. As both a bio mom and a stepmom, I can tell you that both roles are incredibly difficult. Not all bio moms are difficult or off their hinges. I have appreciation for all women who try their best to care for our next generation. I can also honestly tell you that stepmomming is MUCH more difficult. There are not many resources out there that talk about the realities and provide women with the platforms they need to release their frustration and gain some reprieve. In this book I will talk about the many ways our society has created such an unforgiving role for these women. I will use anecdotes from my own life as a stepmom to unpack all the ways our experiences as stepmothers relate and ultimately, how I found my peace in this role. I love being a stepmom, but I do not judge those who have not yet found their footing or the love of the role. It is *damn* hard, and it was a challenge for me to get to where I am today.

What is a stepmom? Or *who* is a stepmom? I think it is important for us to look at and acknowledge the real women behind the role so that we can really understand the daily lives and even traumas of these women. A stepmom is a woman who chooses to love and care for another woman's child like her own. It seems simple enough, except she is constantly living in a world of contradiction where she is told to "know her place," to "not overstep," to "love more," to "stay out of it," all while being expected to feed, clothe, bathe, cuddle, soothe, and show unconditional love for her stepchildren. The relationship between a stepmom and bio mom can, and *does*, really impact the life of the stepmom on various levels. This relationship can impact a stepmother's relationship with her stepchildren and even her relationship with her partner, whom I will refer to as bio dad. While everyone around her are adults responsible for their own actions, thoughts, and feelings, the bio mom has the ability to really set the tone for the future of her and her children's family. She has been blessed by society with the upper hand and if allowed, can wield it in any direction.

Perhaps this book should be titled "Surviving Stepmomming." There are plenty of times that it feels like that is all we are doing, *surviving*. The more stepmoms I talk to, the more I have come to realize that we are all in this together. Our struggles are not unique or rare and our emotions and feelings are not abnormal. This is a simple realization I wish I had figured out a little earlier in my journey. I am not alone. You are not alone. We are all just trying to survive. Now, that is not to say that we do not enjoy being mothers to our stepchildren, but this book is not about validating the love we have for our children. We work every day, trying to prove our love for our children. Something a bio mom never has to do. Instead, this book is an unapologetic expression of emotion that I hope can give voice to the amazing women who wake up every day and *choose* to love and *choose* to mother. Afterall, these women did not birth these babies. These women have no legal responsibilities to these children given by birth and yet, they choose to care for these little humans no matter what obstacles or hardships are thrown their way. These women are warriors who deserve to be validated.

This book is not a magical "how to" guide to all things stepmomming. I cannot pretend that I have all the answers. I am not sure any of us really do. What works for one momma may not work for another. What works in one family dynamic, may not work in all dynamics. Stepmomming is a lifelong journey in self-discovery and self-evolution. Nothing is forever, everything is temporary. The struggles of today will be gone tomorrow, or at least some day in the future. While I still experience challenges, whether through inconsiderate decision making by bio parents, rude comments, or changing family dynamics, I have found peace in my role as stepmom. In fact, through acceptance, I have found the happiness and beauty in stepmomming!

I recently saw a post in one of my many social media-based stepmom support groups in which a young stepmom spoke about how she became friends with her stepchild's bio mom. The author credited herself and her above and beyond love for her stepchild for the great relationship she and bio mom now share. She boasted that she had reached out to bio mom, sat and spoke with her, allowing bio mom to ask her questions until bio mom grew comfortable. There was an air of "*you could do this too, if only you loved your child more.*" This post made me roll my eyes. What this book will not do is assume that I understand all the intricacies of one stepmom's relationship with her child's bio mom. It is not always so cut and dry. I will not preach about the importance of "winning over" bio mom or "trying harder." I am not a psychologist writing about a five-point system to become besties with bio mom. For some stepmoms, this is just not ever going to be a reality. I will not judge you for not sharing a relationship with bio mom. Afterall, this relationship must be reciprocated. You cannot force someone to be friendly with you, no matter how hard we may try.

What this book *is*, is an opportunity for me to share my journey to happiness and validate and affirm the feelings of the women who choose to be stepmoms. These are feelings that are so often tucked away deep within the heart and soul of the stepmomming woman. These are feelings she is not allowed to voice unless she wants to invite criticism for her "lack of love" or "inability to be a parent." What others do not realize about these women, however, is that they are fierce. They are tireless. They are selfless. They are lovers. And they are *human*. These women deserve to have their feelings heard. For the majority, they are not "evil stepmothers" trying to take the place of bio mom. They are not trying to "brainwash" their stepchildren. To what end? For what benefit? They are simply trying to live their lives with their chosen partner and ensure their stepchildren's happiness as best they can. They are not superhuman and they endure struggle. This book is for all the real *women* behind the smiling mask. I see you. I am you. You aren't crazy. You are *killing it!*

My Story

As of this very moment, I am a stepmom to a wonderful stepdaughter, and bio mom to three wonderful bio children, ages nine years, four years, three years, and 1.5 years. My husband and I live with our children in the suburbs of Northern Virginia on the outskirts of Washington, D.C., where we live a relatively normal and peaceful existence. It was not always this way. I became a stepmom before I became a bio mom. I met my now husband when his daughter was six months old. He was living in Virginia while his daughter lived in New Jersey with her mother. When I met my husband, he was still trying to figure out his co-parenting relationship with his daughter's mother. The wounds of a failed relationship were still open despite the decision to move apart. We truly had a whirlwind courtship. In that first week, we spent almost every moment together. We found comfort in one another and I think we both knew early on that this was it. He checked off everything I could have hoped for in a partner. So, when he first told me he had a daughter, I did not spend too much time thinking what that really meant. I asked a few standard questions about the situation, for instance, what's her name, what's going on with her mom, but I didn't pry too deeply. I was happy and in love. Perhaps part of me didn't want to spoil it. Perhaps I was just naïve about the whole situation.

When I first started spending time with my now bonus baby around her first birthday, it was not well received by her bio mom. At the time, I empathized with her bio mom, trying to imagine how unideal this situation was for her and how difficult it must have been to "share" her child with another woman. I made efforts to reach out and be amicable. To my shock, my efforts were NOT well received. In hindsight, perhaps the offer came too soon, too quickly. Scabs were still healing, and bio dad and bio mom were still trying to work it all out. Unscathed, I left an open invitation for us, at any point in life, to try again. In my *very* naïve mind, we were still going to be besties that watch each other's kids when one of us needed a break, let loose together on a Saturday night while bio dad watched the kids, get Sunday morning coffee… you get the idea. In reality, she hated me, hated bio dad, and made it well known. Those first few years were hell and I really questioned just what-the-fuck I was doing. I went from single nights out with my girls, fun dates with my then boyfriend-now husband, to custody battles, screaming babies, and a stressed and crumbling relationship with my partner. The change took place in what seemed like an instant. Life was happening and I kept moving along, going through the motions all while wondering if this was "worth it." Was my relationship worth THIS? Was it worth the stress? Was it worth another woman hating me? Was it worth becoming a mom overnight? Was it worth the emotional exhaustion of supporting my boyfriend as he fought for time with his kid, not knowing if in the end we would even be able to make this relationship work? Would there always be some sort of rift or third party between us? As I fast forward to today, and reflect on the last eight and a half years, I am grateful that I stuck it out. My stepdaughter is now nine. My then boyfriend is now my husband. We have two biological sons together and one biological daughter. We live a comfortable, fun life and I *love* my family. To think that I almost allowed the emotions and actions of other people change my own personal life choices is devastating. It is a lesson I almost had to learn the hard way when at one point during the last eight and a half years, I HAD separated from my husband (pre-marriage) with no certainty that I would ever see him or my bonus baby again. From my journey, I have learned two very important things. When forming a blended household, the behavior of the children's bio mom can have a real impact on the family, but even more importantly, the behavior of your partner *toward* bio mom will really make or break the foundation. Being a bio mom in a co-parenting situation is by no means easy. It takes a lot of courage, empathy, consciousness, self-awareness, and selflessness. A bio mom's actions absolutely set the tone for the future of her children's families. The bio mom will always be "mom." She will always have the upper hand, legally, emotionally, and morally within society. Society will never label her the "evil mom" as they do stepmoms. They will never say she is acting immaturely, as they do stepmoms. Even the most hostile of bio moms will still hear the toxic excuse "but, she *is* still mom," as if birthing a baby innately makes a person worthy of that child's life.

I wanted to write a book that captures a representation of the experiences of the hundreds of thousands of women who are choosing to take on this once extremely taboo and highly criticized role of stepmom. I am not looking to throw shade on bio moms, bio dads, or stepdads. The role of a stepmom is complicated, nuanced, and stigmatized in our western culture. It is not often spoken about and when it is, it is spoken from the perspective of society, psychologists, and bio moms. Stepmoms are given advice for how to be better stepmoms, how to be better co-parents for bio moms, how to be better support to bio dad. When I was struggling with my role and identity as a stepmom, I felt alone and unvalidated. As if I was wrong for wanting a relationship with my chosen partner or wanting to be a loving adult figure to my stepdaughter. It seemed like the sentiment and all the literature was telling me that bio dad should just be alone for the rest of his life otherwise risk upsetting bio mom. And I, the stepmom, was the problem, and my feelings did not matter. Quite frankly, that is bullshit. I am a woman and a human just like bio mom and bio dad. I have thoughts, feelings, needs, and desires. I now know I was not and am not alone. It is time for us as women to step into the light, to express ourselves, correct the narrative, and simply hear from one another that our experiences are not abnormal, not even the unpleasant ones unfortunately.

I hope I can use my story and my journey to help others who are struggling with their stepmom identity, whether new to the game or just never having figured it out fully. Some of these stories will be raw and difficult to hear. Some may offer no real advice, but rather just serve as my own venting session to showcase the similarities across our lives as stepmoms. I hope some of this can make you laugh, and I hope you can walk away from this book knowing, you are *not* crazy, sis.

A Brief but Highly Relevant History of Women in Western Society

We need to talk about the history of women, their identities as mothers and the shifting dynamics we are currently experiencing in our society. Quite simply, the roles of women in America and western society are changing. Our society is evolving. We are beginning to recognize and accept the many identities and roles that have existed within women and played by women for centuries. The care giver, the bread winner, the pioneer, the stability, the emotional, and the unemotional. Women have been kings, pharaohs, business owners and CEOs. We have ruled from behind the curtains and have raised generations after generations. Yet, these are seen as the outliers and our breadth of knowledge, skill, and abilities have still gone largely unacknowledged in present day society. While our post 2020 shift has brought a whole new world of opportunity to American women, it has also brought a world battling with tradition, evolution, and contradiction. The latest 2020 US Census tells us there are an estimated 85 *million* mothers in the US. This does not include the estimated 1.6 million people who did not participate in the 2020 census, some of which I am willing to bet were mothers struggling with child care, work, and sanitization through the pandemic and were just a smidge too busy to remember to complete a census form. You know, just holding the country together during a global pandemic, no big deal. So, now that there are all these grand new opportunities and adventures open to women, millennial and Generation Z women are still juggling the responsibilities of motherhood AND trying to prove themselves with other equally fulfilling and meaningful roles. Personally, I am a full-time bio mom, stepmom, corporate executive, entrepreneur, wife, sister, health nut… and dare I say, author? All while expected to continue doing most of the unpaid labor in my house, family, and community. As humans, all these different roles go into creating our identities. I do not believe that any one of these alone can define us. If they did, we would constantly be feeling like either a pure failure or a pure success and as non-Y chromosome humans, let's be honest, we tend to skew toward the feelings of failure rather than success. In our society, women have a difficult time accepting success that does not come in the way of motherhood or anything less than two hundred percent in all areas of our lives. But why is this? How have we allowed our society, controlled by men, to so strongly influence our self-identities, our self-confidence, and our self-definitions? At one point in human history, societies worshipped women and even associated women with power. The ancient Sumerians, one of the earliest recorded civilizations, worshipped goddesses like Inanna who was associated with things like sex, love, beauty, war, justice, and political power. Ancient Sumerian women could own property, run businesses, becomes priests and judges, and even serve as witnesses in court – which was a big deal back in the day. Even the ancient Romans and Greeks worshiped female goddesses alongside male gods. However, over the course of human history, women began to lose their stature in society. The modern Christian bible recounts the story of Jesus' resurrection, in which it is written that four women witnessed the rising of Jesus. However, it was not until a man verified these claims that the women were believed. Somewhere between ancient Sumer and the birth of Christianity, women had lost their credibility as witnesses, could no longer own property, and in essence became the property of men. Perhaps as the world began to shrink, and men became thirsty for power, seizing and plundering neighboring civilizations, the attributes of women as lovers, diplomats, child bearers, healers, all things once cherished, became second to survival from these raids and war. Instead, societies needed strong warriors to protect their homelands, bringing a rise to male authority. As time went on, the hold and control of women continued. Despite all their power and glory, men still needed women to reproduce, carry-on family lines, and produce new warriors. We can still see the battle going on today around female reproductive rights in America, where a majority-white male Congress try to make female centric, reproductive laws and decisions that benefit males over females. In America, Salem, Massachusetts is famously known for their 1600s witch hunts against females. Females who were too outspoken, too powerful, too threatening to the patriarchal structure designed to keep men in power were burned and drowned as witches. Centuries of female inferiority and female idealisms created by males *for males* has brought us to a modern-day society that tells women to "stay in their places," to "smile more," to "marry a doctor, or a lawyer" versus "push the boundaries" or "study hard to be a doctor or a lawyer." This rhetoric pits women against one another in the belief that there is only room for one female executive amongst a team of males, or that one lousy female professional could "ruin it for the rest of us." Up until 2020, this male centric ideal told women to rely on men to protect us, provide for us, to cook and clean and be doting wives and mothers to keep men happy. Finally, we are beginning to see a resurrection of female empowered movements like the #METOO movement and Black Lives Matter. We are experiencing a transition in our society where women are playing a leading role. Women are slowly encouraging other women to be successful careerists, hobbyists, entrepreneurs, and politicians. We are ever so slowly empowering one another in most things, except motherhood. And why is that? How are we to progress as an empowered population if we remain so critical of other women's parenting choices?

Perhaps motherhood is not so simple anymore and perhaps even we, women, need time to adjust. In today's America, about fifty percent of families are blended with a stepparent. These re-coupled relationships have a sixty-seventy percent failure rate, which is much higher than the thirty-forty percent failure rate of non-recoupled or remarried relationships. There are endless studies to tell us why this is the case, but any step parent can tell you that as hard as marriage is, a marriage that involves already existing children with already existing dynamics and a third party is HIGHLY complex. Furthermore, The Stepfamily Foundation Inc. tells us that 1,300 new stepfamilies are forming every day. So, within this fifty percent – and growing number of re-coupled partnerships – are millions of millennial and Gen Z women contemplating their life choices every day as stepmoms. I know. I was one of them. The constant fighting with bio mom and feeling that I was responsible for another woman's misery really wore me down. Looking back on it, I wish I had questioned myself as to why I was holding myself responsible for her emotions and actions. Afterall, I wasn't there when her relationship ended nor am I responsible for another adult's emotions or actions. Nevertheless, I was falling victim to society's stigmas that stepmothers are evil homewreckers, as opposed to asking why bio mom was dragging me into the middle of her own struggles with her insecurities and why bio dad – my now husband – was allowing it to happen. Why as women, can we not lift one another and support one another? Why do we allow jealousy to win out and pin us against one another when we already have a whole society doing it for us?

Aside from the constant critiques, there is a truly unique dichotomy only experienced by the women who are known as stepmom. Despite all our societal evolution that claims to acknowledge a woman's worth beyond her motherhood, coupled with the fact that a stepmomming woman did not physically birth their children, our society still expects a stepmom to fulfill her pre-defined female gender duties. Stepmoms are expected to care for the family and tend to the house. Husbands and boyfriends with children often rely on their wives and girlfriends to nurture their biological children, be on top of activity schedules, and keep a clean house. These stepmomming women are expected to love and be maternal to children they did not birth and in some instances met later in the child's adolescent life. These women are held to the same expectation of any female who has birthed a child, even though they have not. I should be clear, many stepmoms do not mind filling this role. Many women do have the maternal instincts to care for her home and family and many of us millennial women are the cusp generation of social change where we were still raised as mothers and wives. And for the women unable to have their own biological children, being a stepmother can be magical. The uniqueness in this dichotomy comes from the converse opinion where society says that there *is* a such thing, as a stepmother showing *too* much love to their stepchildren. So, while stepmomming women are expected to fulfill the quintessential motherly roles, she is not, however, supposed to love her babies to the point of "real" motherhood. To sum it up, stepmothers are expected to be maternal to their stepchildren, but only the "right amount" of maternal. They are expected to sacrifice, love, and mend, but only to the levels that others find appropriate.

Harsh Realities and Facing Them Straight On

I am just going to say it. Not everyone is meant to be a stepmom! The basic fact is that stepmomming is HARD, complicated, and complex. At any given point in time, a stepmom can be and will be pulled in completely opposite directions. There will be unrealistic and pluralistic expectations of this woman. There will be critics demeaning her, at times she will feel like an outsider in her own home, and hardly anyone will ever give her the praise she deserves. Along her journey, she will be labeled many different things. Some good, some not so good. She will find herself playing the role of the "mediator." At least once in her life, she is likely to be accused of coming "in between" bio dad and bio mom in some way. She will almost certainly be told that she is "over-stepping" and almost just as certainly, she will be told that she doesn't care enough, doesn't love enough, isn't involved enough, is simply "not enough." A stepmom will be labeled many things. As a stepmom, a woman can never just "be." What would she be? She cannot be "mom." There already is a mom. But she *must* be *something*. As a society, we are obsessed with making a stepmom fit into a role in a traditional familial system that does not actually have a place for a stepmom. While we praise men who "step up" to be stepdads, we hold their female counterparts in contempt. We tell stepdads how amazing they are for taking on another man's children. We hail them as heroes for loving a single mom and accepting her children, as though this woman is otherwise not worthy of love. As far as we have come in a post 2020 world, we still struggle to fully free women from their gender stigmas.

Women who stepmom are constantly labeled and criticized in some way, shape, or form. The most difficult part about these various roles of a stepmom, is that you will never truly know when or how you will be labeled, and you will always be managing two opposing dynamics. There is the stepchild to bio dad relationship and the bio dad to bio mom relationship. After 8.5 years of stepmomming, I have just now fully accepted that no matter what I do, it most likely is not going to be "right." I have realized that I may *think* I am choosing the right action in the moment, but I will most likely be wrong. I may get it right within one dynamic but get it completely wrong on the other. Which leads me to what a stepmom is not. Do you know what a stepmom is not? What I am not? Stepmoms are not mind readers! Despite our amazing empathy and abilities to care for another woman's child, we lack the superhuman ability to read anyone's mind. GASP! SHOCKER! Lacking the ability of telepathy makes it rather difficult to understand how our partners wish for us to respond in any given situation, which more often than not, leads to hurt feelings, disappointment, and failed expectations all around. It also makes it hard to guess what our significant others' feelings toward bio mom's parenting skills are on any given day. In my experience, this can change like the wind. One moment bio mom is "a terrible mom," and the next she's "just struggling, and we should give her a break." Can I sign up for a break? When do I get my stepmom break? I'm pretty sure bio mom is getting her bio mom break while the kids are here with us… Regardless of who gets a break and when, why are stepmoms held to such high standards when bio moms are accepted as simply being… moms?

No one is blaming the bio mom for her irrational reactions, missed opportunities, or over stepping into others' lives. Why do we expect stepmoms to be super humans? Super moms? To constantly have emotions in check, to constantly know the right things to say, to consistently provide for all of those in her life. Stepmothers are expected to cook, clean, cuddle, and care but without overstepping into the lane of "mom." Stepmoms are often expected to do all the unpaid labor that generally falls into the realm of responsibility for the female gender role in western society with very little in return. Bio mothers often face the same expectations, however, have the added result of gratitude, kisses, hugs, and praise, all things that do not come regularly to stepmoms. I have met countless stepmoms who can consciously recount a, or *the* time their stepchild actually showed them affection or gratitude. This is not to say we expect our children to be anything more than children or to be attuned to our feelings. What I'm saying is, it'd be nice to get a happy mother's day/stepmother's day craft sent home from school every once in a while. Unlike most biomothers, these events of affection do not happen often for many stepmoms. So, when they do, they mean the world to us and we can recount almost every time it has happened.

    The role of a stepmom is exhausting. There is not a day that goes by that I do not reflect on the events of the day and try to make sense of my role, my partner's expectations, and what went right and what went wrong. The first:

    The "mediator." Time and time again I have had to play this role between my husband and my bonus baby. The thing is, this is not all that much different from being a bio mom. As a bio mom, my husband and I parent our bio children equally. Whenever one of us is disciplining our children or on them for misbehaving, the other is usually a calming force, balancing out the situation and preventing unnecessary escalation. It is kind of a natural yin and yang. As a stepmom, however, this situation is so much more complex. Generally speaking, *most* situations are so much more complex as a stepmom! Stepmoms are first off, not meant to discipline, even if the child lacks any other discipline in his or her life. We are simply supposed to allow our stepchildren to run wild, go to bed whenever they feel like it, chew with their mouths open, be generally horrid little creatures, and not have an opinion about it. Excuse the sarcasm here, but this drives me fucking wild. Early on in my journey with my now husband and bonus baby I learned this the more difficult way. I am naturally a nurturer and naturally a mediator both at home and in the workplace. I enjoy taking two or more parties in conflict and bridging gaps to bring about amicable closures and solutions. It is one of my characteristics and abilities that I believe has brought me professional success as a consultant in the corporate world. I also think it is one of my personality traits that my husband really appreciated within me. So, it was almost inevitable that my husband's expectation of my natural savior, mediator disposition would eventually clash with my, perhaps less favorable, type A personality. My type A personality can also be held partly responsible for my professional success in a male dominated industry. It may also be the reason I crave structure and desire scheduling, and discipline. While I am naturally an empath, I have personal expectations for structure both within myself and my family. I have had to learn over the years to let go of parts of these desires and expectations. Stepmomming can sometime mean sacrificing parts of ourselves, usually the less favorable parts, for the greater good of a balanced at home dynamic and our overall personal happiness. It's a constant internal battle over the lesser of two evils, so the speak. Trying to enforce bedtimes or behavioral expectations often led to disagreements with my husband and quite frankly, was changing the relationship I had with my bonus baby. It just wasn't worth it. While I cannot be expected to be the mediator and calming force *every* time my husband and stepdaughter have disciplinary moments, I have made the conscious choice to be a light and neutral presence in my stepdaughter's life. Children will show their bio moms unconditional love through good times and bad. Stepmothers do not get that same unconditional love. So instead of risking the loss of my stepdaughter's love, I have chosen to "loosen up" a bit, which I am okay with because I made this decision for myself. No one told me to do it and it works for my situation where my stepdaughter has two living and participating bio parents. It is not always fair, and it is certainly not always easy to walk away or to pass matters onto my husband, but hey that's stepmomming.

The "in between." This one may be my favorite. Inevitably, many stepmoms will be accused of being the problem or trying to come in between bio dad and bio mom. This accusation may be lobbed over the wall from bio mom, may come from your bedside from a stressed out and perhaps emotionally exhausted bio dad, or even come from high up in the stands hurled through the crowd by a third party. When it comes from bio dad, it is whole heartedly a signal that the energy is on the wrong mom. As a stepmom, I get it. Co-parenting is a fickle relationship. I have seen how quickly it can turn negative or even hostile. I can understand that any tip in balance can threaten the whole eco system. Which is why this phrase may pop up at a time when stepmom believes she is correctly supporting her partner, bio dad, by validating his actions or even just simply agreeing with him and his feelings, most likely in the privacy of her own home. She may suddenly get hit with something similar to "why are you trying to be in between us?" Um… excuse me? Last time I checked, I wasn't the one holding your children hostage for more child support. Which is a perfect example of an inside thought most stepmoms will never voice out loud. Rather we recognize the emotional turmoil in our partners' lives and excuse the outburst.

The first time I got hit with this one was after years of a very toxic custody negotiation. We had been in and out of court so many times, it was almost like a second home. I was taking time off from work to attend and support my now husband for what seemed like weekly court dates. Dates in which bio mom would choose not to show up forcing rescheduling after we had already made the three-and-a-half-hour drive from Virginia to New Jersey for the eight a.m. appearance. Or for court dates that resulted in the judge telling bio mom and bio dad to "try to work it out, come back if you can't," which of course resulted in us coming back only two weeks later when they could not work it out. I also rode shot gun from Virginia to New Jersey to all the pickups and drop-offs, with many "pickups" ending with us coming home empty handed because bio mom decided not to show. Despite all the time, stress, and missed work, I was standing by my husband because I believed in our team. I believed he *should* be in his daughter's life. I believed he was doing the right thing to keep showing up despite the let downs and rescheduling. I would let him vent about bio mom and most always supported his position. At times when I did not agree, I either delicately stated alternate perspectives or just held my tongue altogether figuring that he was speaking out of emotion and it was not worth an argument. It was not until almost five years into the legal battles and our first bio child together, that I had truly started to have enough of bio mom's influence over my husband's emotions. Emotions that would spill over into our own family dynamics. I was tired of hearing about her, tired of talking about her, tired of all the grief she had tried to put our family through. I was grappling with my own pent up emotions, emotions that had been simmering for five years that were now beginning to boil. So, imagine my surprise when my husband did a one hundred and eighty degree turn one day and started spewing out excuses for bio mom and her behavior. In that moment, I felt immediately undervalued, ignored, and irrelevant. It felt as if my husband was not aware of the emotional distress, she had put on ME and our relationship for FIVE YEARS. I had to say something. In my most calm and diplomate like voice I could muster in the moment, I reminded my husband of all the hurt and anguish we had been through only to end up with limited time with our daughter. That's when, for the first time, I heard it. My husband said some *bullshit* like "why are you trying to come in between *us?*" In that moment, for him to refer to himself and bio mom as "*us*" signified to me that I was thought of as the outsider. Despite our new bio baby and marriage, my husband was still putting his energy into his relationship – however good or bad – with my stepdaughter's mother. I was crushed. Simultaneously he was telling me that he was taking my love and support for absolute-fucking-granted. He was so comfortable in my identity as his support person rather than his wife, partner, co-parent, equal human engaged in a consensual cohabitating relationship, that my mere disagreement threw a total glitch in his reality. We have since worked through these situations and feelings and after some heated words in that moment, we were able to speak rationally and work through what was very obvious to me, a brief moment of insanity on his part. I did, however, learn from that experience that as much time and energy my husband and I invest into our relationship and teaming, we experience bio mom differently. I realized that although we shared similar experiences with bio mom, we each react differently, we process differently, we channel our stress differently, we perceive differently, and for that reason it is usually never worth sharing my opinion in the moment. I now prefer to take time away to process my thoughts and feelings to be sure I am providing the right guidance for my husband and our family. Looking back on our journey, I recognize that everything we go through is temporary. Bio mom can have her ups and downs. My husband can also have his ups and downs. None of it will last forever and some of it just isn't worth my energy.

The "over stepper and not enough." Ah, the over stepper and not enough. Oxymorons that a stepmom will often here. But let me ask, if you aren't "overstepping," are you even stepmomming? I kid. Overstepping is, quite simply, when a stepmom is accused of loving her stepchild too much. Stepmoms are usually told by bio mom, sometimes even bio dad, and others that she is overstepping. What bio mom is really saying is that she is threatened by stepmom's loving and positive presence in her child's life. What bio dad is really saying is that he is also threatened but in different ways. Perhaps he is afraid of blowback from bio mom. Perhaps he is afraid of losing his theoretical position as the "preferred" parent to the children. Whatever it is, it is deeply rooted in an insecurity that we, as stepmothers, cannot control. What I have learned is that it is easy for a woman to feel like she is being replaced or "out done" by a stepmother. Personally, I have never wanted to be "better than" nor have I ever wanted to "out do" my bonus baby's bio mother. I simply want to be the best version of myself for my stepchild. What is comical is that while one person is complaining that I may be "overstepping" another can be complaining that I am not doing *enough*. The dueling dynamics and accusations can be exhausting. Damned if you do, damned if you don't. There was a time I enforced bedtimes, I did my bonus baby's hair, I fed, taught, and straight up mommed my stepdaughter. I noticed that it began to create an odd imbalance in my relationship with my husband. Outside influences and societal norms told my husband and I that as a female presence, I should do all these things. Woman should *want* to be involved with children. Woman *should* be loving and nurturing. They *should* be the primary caretakers of the children in the house. This may have worked during a time that families were nuclear and women mainly took up professions as stay at home mothers, but this gender-based expectation does not take into account split family dynamics. Our stepdaughter was only with us a fraction of the time, which meant my husband only got so much time to bond and parent. My assumed responsibility robbed my husband of his time to truly parent and bond with his daughter. I began seeing him push back on my efforts to regulate my stepdaughter's sleep schedule or other mundane decisions. I started getting frustrated that my husband was not only not supporting my parenting, but drastically moving in the opposite direction. So, I stopped parenting. I slowly began withdrawing from bed-time routines, morning hair brushing, bath times, and food conversations. The petty side of me thought "if you want to be a single dad, you can be a single dad." While the more mature side of me saw this for what it was, which I perceived to be a man desperate for some influence into the upbringing of his daughter. All was going fine for a while. I had found a new groove and a new role in my stepdaughter's life, with which I was happy. I was finally becoming the fun stepmom! I could pass tough and unfavorable decisions off to dad and almost always be the good guy. I would sometimes have to witness my husband make wrong decisions that would stir up unnecessary drama, but I had learned to ignore it and keep it moving. Of course, this wasn't exactly ideal. I would have preferred a more balanced dynamic where my husband was the primary parent, but I still had *some* say. For some reason it was an all or nothing for us and we had swayed from a single stepmom mentality to a single dad mentality where only one of us parented autonomously. So, I went with it. It seemed to be what my husband wanted and after all, it is his bio kid. This went on for some time before my husband made the claim that I was now not involved enough. By this time, he was exhausted both mentally and physically from doing it all on his own. It hurt. With little to no communication from him, I truly thought I had been doing the right thing this time. I had been following his lead! I was the fun stepmom that he told me I should be! After a few months' worth of mostly bitter discussions, we finally began to transition into the much more balanced parenting approach we have today. I do not currently feel the need to parent and interfere in everything with my bonus baby, I will still let my husband do a lot of the heavy lifting, but I also feel more empowered to be involved. *HE* makes me feel more empowered to be involved recognizing that he cannot do it all on his own.

HCBM

High Conflict Bio Mom

I mean, what is there to say? When you know, you know. I think only those of us who have dealt with the HCBM truly know what living a nightmare may feel like. I'd like to believe that those women dealing with a high conflict bio parent are just paying their dues for eternal bliss. Could heaven just be a world where high conflict parenting doesn't exist, and everyone co-parents peacefully in their separate homes with agreed upon boundaries and bedtimes? A place where all parties are respected and passive-aggressive Facetime calls are immediately disconnected?

I am not totally sure what exactly I was expecting the first time I met my stepdaughter's bio mom. I was nervous. I desperately wanted her to like me. My husband, then boyfriend, told me they were "cool." I should have known right there that this was not going to go well. If a man ever sums up his relationship with a female as "we're cool" they are either A. more than "cool" or B. definitely *not* cool. Perhaps this is a slight exaggeration or generalization, but I find that this presumptive approach keeps me safe. I knew there had been some apprehension on bio mom's part leading up to our meeting. There had been a lot of back and forth on the decision, but from my perspective she had ultimately decided she wanted to meet the other woman in her child's life. What could go wrong? Things seemed rational. If I was in her shoes, I would absolutely want to meet the other woman my child was spending time around. I would absolutely want to have a relationship with that person, if only to keep an eye on things. So, to me, all of this made sense! My husband was planning on dropping off his daughter with her bio mom at a Walgreens parking lot in New Jersey and I tagged along for the three-and-a-half-hour ride from Virginia. This would be the beginning to a very long pick up/drop off drama filled saga. A saga that could rival any of the Greek classics or Shakespearean plays.

When we arrived at the location, I jumped out to use the restroom inside the store. See the part where we had been driving for three and a half hours and bio mom was not yet there. She lived nearby and so naturally, had to be late for the agreed upon time. As I came naively walking out of the store and closer to my partner's car, I quickly realized that something was not right. She didn't seem to notice me or to be looking for me in any way. Looking back on the situation, it was pretty clear that my partner had perhaps not mentioned that I was there. Just an overall bad move on the part of my boyfriend. Once my daughter's bio mom acknowledged me and realized the situation, her reaction… was not favorable. In the event of my stepdaughter ever reading this book, I will leave it there. It led to the beginning of a *very* long legal battle in and out of family court.

Unfortunately, this story is NOT unusual. Why, as women, can we not appreciate other women? Aside from the understandable initial shock, bio mom and I have had eight and a half, almost nine very long years of co-existence in my stepdaughter's life and very little acceptance or appreciation. Why do we hate rather than uplift? Why is it that men can accept stepfathers into their children's lives much more easily than women?

A high conflict bio mother has the innate ability to destroy your relationship, your mental peace, have you questioning your life choices, and wonder just where civilization has gone so wrong. What I have learned from my dealings with my stepdaughter's bio mom, is that these women act this way because they feel a loss of control. Similar to our role as stepmothers, bio mothers going through this transition feel an insecurity around letting go of their children or maybe even *losing* them to someone else. Once I accepted this realization, bio mom's behavior became easier to ignore. Of course, the court and legal fees did not become any easier to ignore, but I was finally able to sympathize with her grieving which in turn brought me much more mental peace.

I do not think there is anything in the universe that has the potential to make a HCBM more high conflict than the idea of her children calling another woman "mom." It doesn't matter if that bio mom is actively involved, not actively involved, negligent, or mother of the year. As women, it is hard to hear such a special title be given by our children to another woman. It seems to be powerful enough to make a previously sane person crazy. Bio moms will make claims that bio dad or stepmom have "brainwashed" her children into calling their stepmother "mom," or wait, maybe it was hypnotism…Personally, neither my husband nor I have ever *forced* my stepdaughter to call me "mom." For the first four years of our lives together, my husband always referred to me by my first name when talking to my stepdaughter. There never seemed to be a big issue. As my stepdaughter got a little older, she started asking questions about names and titles. She was curious. Of course, I told her that she could refer to me with whatever name or title she was comfortable. She tried out "mom" a bit, but even at such a young age was sensitive to the overt feelings of her bio mother, so quickly stopped using it. Once my bio children were born and began talking, things slowly changed. While my husband and I would still refer to me by my first name, my stepdaughter would use my first name and "mom" interchangeably. She understood that I am her stepmother, but also was a kid who just wanted to "fit in" with her siblings. This led to several conversations from bio mom to both bio dad and I and my stepdaughter. Following that period, my stepdaughter felt the need to make it clear in her actions and words that she knew I was her stepmom and *not* her bio mom. Now at the age of nine, she makes sure to introduce me to people as her *step*mom and to talk to her bio mother about her *step*mom. Meanwhile, she has increasingly referred to me as "mom" when we are together, which I think helps her truly feel at home with her siblings. As a mother, I refuse to ask her to refrain from doing something that makes her feel happy and could risk making her feel negatively singled out of the family. I will, however, occasionally take a moment to remind her that no matter what she wishes to call me, she will always be my first baby and will always be a part of this family. I remind her that no matter who may choose to be upset, neither she nor I can control their feelings. Which is a life lesson I often have to remind myself.

I have heard from plenty of stepmoms who do not allow their stepchildren to call them "mom" because they see it as disrespectful to bio mom. While this is a respectable choice, I cannot say I agree with it. If a child is trying to create a bond with their stepmother or has created that bond with their stepmother, why damage their little egos? To a kid, it's almost like saying "I like you, kid, but not *that* much." From a stepmom perspective, I get it. It can be extremely uncomfortable for a child that you did not birth to call you "mom." When I first experienced it, I had to really reflect on my feelings. I did not want to put up a wall between my bonus baby and me. At the same time, I did not want to deal with the drama from bio mom, or the many questions from strangers. I did not want people to think I wanted to "take credit" for this child – even though I was doing all the motherly duties similar to any other mother and quite frankly felt as though I did deserve the title of "mom." Ultimately, though, I realized that most of the discomfort I felt was coming from factors and people outside of my relationship with my stepdaughter. It really had nothing to do with my feelings toward my stepdaughter or the relationship we had formed. It was all centered around fear of judgment, or fear of upsetting others, and even a feeling of unworthiness. For me, however, that relationship that I share with my stepdaughter has and always will take priority. I cannot be responsible for other people's comfort or understanding. That said, it can be a challenge to overcome these insecurities and fears. Over the years I have found that keeping my focus on my relationship with my child really helps reduce the outside noise. My focus as a stepmom is being the best, most positive, and most loving woman I can be for my stepdaughter. I want her to feel just as much a part of her dad's side of her family as my bio children. If calling me "mom" helps make her feel happy, then I will gladly deal with any fall out. Or I just won't deal with it at all. Quite honestly, this topic would likely fall under the category of "don't engage" for me. I cannot control the relationship bio mom has with my stepdaughter, nor can I control the relationship my husband has with my stepdaughter. Everyone is responsible for cultivating their own relationships and whatever they cultivate is theirs to live with. All I can control is me and giving the most that I can to my own relationship with my stepdaughter.

Not every stepmom will agree with my opinion on this topic. And guess what? That is okay! There are no right and wrong answers. Stepmomming is a gray area, it is not black and white. As long as the children are at the forefront of all decisions, then it is the "right" decision. Let's normalize acceptance and even making mistakes. As women trying to navigate the white-water rapids of stepmomming with nothing more than a small row boat, we should try better to support one another. Let's ask ourselves, "what do I get for criticizing another stepmom?", "is what she is doing really that bad?" Most of the time, the answer is no, it's not that bad. Afterall what is true for most of us doing this parenting thing, is that most of our decisions are shaky at best and regrettable at worst, step parents and bio parents alike.

If you have not caught on yet, I have a hard time accepting the hierarchical structure of parenting we have in our modern-day culture and how hypocritical our ideals are around gender equality, female rights, and family identity. For better or for worse, our legal codes, policies, and social principles have changed little since the days of stay-at-home moms, "mythical" female orgasms, and fathers who spent more time outside of the house than in. In our society, bio mom reigns above bio dad, stepmom, stepdad, adoptive mom, or any other type of parent really. I do not disagree with a mother's rights to her children. Afterall, she sacrificed her body and in many ways her life to bring her children into the world. She is even expected to continuing sacrificing well into her children's adult lives. We believe that women are more biologically wired to love and care for her children than men. So, we are quick to deem a woman as a "bad mom" while praising a man as a "good father" for doing many of the same things. Men are heralded as "father-of-the-year" for performing mundane tasks, like giving their kids lunch money for school that day. While a woman giving her children lunch money would be judged as a negligent mother who couldn't make her kids a homemade, healthy lunch. I do not ignore the fact that our society still holds all women to very different standards than their male counterparts. Our world of today looks much differently than the world did a few decades ago when many of our legal codes were established. In fact, many of our legal codes and basis of our entire social code has foundations as far back as a few centuries, or even farther back to the pages written in the Bible. That's right, we still operate around the principles found in a 3,500 year old book. Despite my completely useless bachelor's degree in religion, I would say I'm far from an expert in the days of the Bible. Although, I am willing to bet that our lives and our modern society look a little bit different than they did at the time of Jesus. While women can benefit from a system that holds her responsible for our youth and deem her primary worth in society to be procreation and childcare, it often comes at great costs to the vast female population in America in the work place and mental health. While a woman may be more likely to win primary custody of shared children following a divorce, she is less likely to hold an executive level position and she is more likely to suffer from depression. Perhaps we could create a hypothesis that there's some type of correlation between being the default parent and a woman's mental health and professional success. Oh, that's right, those studies exist already and yet we ignore them. When the world shut down for the 2020 COVID-19 pandemic, it was women who were most affected. The number of women who were juggling childcare, at-home learning, work, and sanitation far outnumbered men. Meanwhile, in a post COVID world, we see a rising number of men who are *wanting* to be active fathers.

More men are taking on the role of primary caregiver to their children while their female partners seek employment and high level careers outside of the home *and* openly talk about it. Perhaps it's time to reevaluate how we view gender roles in America and start sharing the burdens and the benefits equally for men and women. Perhaps custody decisions should be made with the children in mind, vice the parents. Perhaps women should not be expected to keep our national economy burning while also raising the next generation solo. And almost certainly, perhaps we should make childcare more accessible and more affordable for all. The idea that rights and responsibilities of child rearing go to the female predates our modern history. For instance, Judaism gets passed down through the mother's line, one school of thought is simply because there was a point in time when DNA and paternity tests did not exist. The most sure-fire way to know if a child was the offspring of a Jewish believer was through the mother who birthed that child. In our current age, we can easily and almost surely determine a person's father through DNA tests. Maury Povich has built an entire stay-home-from-school empire around it. There are subscription services that can tell most people their whole blood line for centuries back. Times have changed. With divorce rates climbing, more American adults choosing to be or forced to be single, and reproduction rates at a continuous low, maybe it's time to look at our reflection, our values, ideals, and policies. Maybe it's time to reevaluate what works for our modern society and what doesn't. When a woman is resisting an amicable co-parenting situation in the unfortunate case of a parental split, we never stop to question why she sees the need to allow her own emotions to put a dark cloud over the lives of her children. We never stop to ask why a woman would make it so difficult for a man who wants to be a parent, to see his children. We almost always ask why that man is not trying harder to see his kids or what did he do to make this woman so angry. While we grant bio mothers near sainthood during custody battles and never question their humanly flaws, we still villainize those same women in other aspects of our system. We criminalize prostitution, locking up victims of sex trafficking, a population that is unsurprisingly disproportionately female. We criminalize abortion, telling rape victims to just deal with the lifelong consequences of their trauma and in the event of life threatening complications, we tell women they should be willing to sacrifice their adult lives for a fetus that may never be compatible with life. Let us not allow the double standards found across our legal codes and policies fool us. These policies are not intended to protect women or other marginalized populations. They are not intended to benefit women. The benefits come as a side effect. And the cost of these double standards and double-edged practices are more fatherless children, more stressed out and depressed mothers, and a strained economy. Until changed, the system will continue preying on the most vulnerable populations of our society, including our women and children.

Protecting the Queen

Creating Boundaries

I quite think the real problem with stepmoms is stepmoms. Hear me out. Most good stepmoms share the same traits. We are consistent. We are responsible. We are unwavering in our commitment and our values. We unintentionally set an expectation that we *are* superhuman. We set an expectation that in the face of any turmoil, we will always hold it down.

Early on in my relationship with my now husband, I found that I was constantly making excuses for him and for bio mom. I was constantly going above and beyond for him and my stepdaughter. I hardly ever thought or spoke about myself. I set us all up to expect such a superhuman level of effort and selflessness that was never going to be sustainable. I did not set boundaries, nor did I set realistic expectations of my emotional and mental tolerance to put up with shit. As a stepmom, I wanted to make everything better. I wanted my partner to be happy. I wanted my stepdaughter to be happy. I really thought I could love them into being happy. The problem is, no one can love anyone else into happiness. Perhaps this was a life lesson I learned FAR too late in life. The countless friends, boyfriends, family that I thought my love could "fix" or make happy, when in reality their happiness wasn't mine to build in the first place. The harder I pushed, the less happy we all got. If happiness is about an individual's perspective of successes, my ideals of happiness cannot always be recreated onto others. Luckily I did learn this early enough in my stepmom journey. Without realizing it at the time, my idea of happiness for my stepdaughter and husband were so tightly linked to an ideal of familial perfection we would and could never achieve. An ideal rooted in a traditional family environment and not based on the realities of being a blended family going through a transitional period where everyone was trying to establish a new normal. Yet, I subconsciously thought I could love us all into happiness. Sometimes loving someone so fiercely actually requires time and distance. Sometimes it means giving breathing space to a person or a problem or a situation. I think as stepmoms we try so hard to fill a void that we *think* we need to fill, but perhaps is not ours to fill. Instead of filling that void, whether it is a neglectful bio mom, a heart-shattered bio dad, a "happy place," maybe instead, we just add something new. As women, we are not here to "fill-in" for someone or something. Instead, we are choosing to add value into our stepchildren's lives. The actions may look very similar. A stepmom caring for her child, giving baths, doing school pick-ups, checking homework, *are* the actions of a mother. But we don't need to fill a void, we really just need to be ourselves. I think all the special traits that make a woman willing and able to stepmom, are the same special traits that can easily drive us to our own failure and exhaustion. We care, perhaps too much at times, we love, perhaps too deeply at times, and we most definitely try too hard most days. Sis, you just have to chill and believe that it will all work out in the end. I promise that it does. For better or for worse, this is all just temporary.

When I first met my husband and he told me he had a daughter, I was totally naïve. In the first few months of dating, I was living in a blissful abyss, floating on rainbows of ice cream outings, cute baby girl clothes, and snuggles. The funny thing about an abyss is there are not many actual rainbows, and it is mostly just a dark vacant hole. Once I woke up from my dream, it did not take long for reality to set in that I was now caring for an actual child. My partner was working nights as a bouncer, often leaving me and my one-year-old bonus baby to fend for ourselves. Overnight, I went from being completely single, focusing on my career, and having fun nights out with my girls, to caring for a tiny human life. As a now bio mom who has gone through the infant to one-year experience with three bio children, I can say that it was so much more difficult with my stepdaughter. There are so many reasons why. As a bio mother you'll often hear from people who have many opinions about many things. Your mother-in-law, your mother, your friends, your co-workers, hell, even the random lady you see at Starbucks while getting your morning coffee will be filled with unsolicited "wisdom" on how you should mother your child. As a bio mom you can choose to filter through the garbage and weed out the nuggets of gold you may want to use or you can simply ignore it all. As a stepmom, you are constantly concerned if what you are doing is right. You constantly wonder if bio mom would approve. You overemphasize the maternal feeling of having to do everything perfectly, one hundred percent of the time. There is little education out there on how to prepare to be a stepmom. You don't read parenting books for fear of being judged or laughed at since all of those books are written for pregnant mothers. For me, the mere fact that I seemingly blinked and found myself lying in bed soothing a *very* unhappy baby night after night was a challenging adjustment. I had traded in bottle service with the girls for baby bottles and spit up. I also wasn't just spending a night with a child, I was caring for my future daughter. I was the woman dating her father. I felt like I had to get everything right. I felt that as the woman, I had to have all the answers despite never having a child of my own. This was "my first go" at caring for a baby. Prior to this, despite some volunteer work I had done with small children, I had never cared for a baby. I had most certainly never cared for a baby in a more-than-baby-sitter, dating-your-daddy, type role. It felt like I never had time to adjust nor did I have the bonding time with my daughter in the same way I would later have with my bio children. There was no prep time. I was saying "put me in, coach" before ever having attended a practice and never expecting to become the star quarterback so quickly. And on top of all of this confusion, self-doubt, and anxiety was a very young child, bouncing around parents and houses, and who was equally as confused as me.

Hey, listen, nothing can really prepare you for those first few weeks, months… years… of motherhood. But… as a bio mom, having a nine-month heads-up filled with cramps, kicks, and sleepless nights is a pretty good prep period. It really helps to get your mind right. Jumping into step parenting was like doing the polar bear plunge during a New England winter. So, when my husband finally recognized how amazing I was (I can confidently say that because I'm a stepmom) and popped the question, I had to dig deep. Sure, I loved this man, and I knew in the depths of my being that this man whole-heartedly loved me. He was not only inviting me into his life, but he was also inviting me into his daughter's life. I also knew that I loved his little girl with all my heart and our connection felt destined. What I had not known was if I was truly capable of giving all of myself to this man and this little girl, willingly taking a second-place seat, and still maintaining my personal happiness.

As little girls we are told to find a partner who will treat us as the center of their universe. *We* are the princesses. We are groomed to believe that the biggest achievements in our lives will come from finding prince charming, convincing prince charming that we are worthy enough to wed and have his children, and then raising his children. While we can now all see the toxicity in these stories and we recognize that we are so much more than our relationship status, it is difficult to fully rid ourselves of these ideals. At the very least, we still want to be the sun in someone's solar system. We still expect to have eyes all on us. As a parent you learn that these behaviors will ebb and flow over the course of your relationship with your partner and your children's lives. There will be times when your needs are at the forefront, other times when your partner's needs are at the forefront, and yet other times when the needs of your children are at the forefront. There will certainly be ups and downs, but overall both you and your partner have equal say in decisions that impact your children. I have learned that as a stepmom you are almost always going to be playing the supporting role to your spouse and child in many situations. That is not to say that your spouse should not care about your feelings and opinions, though. There will just be many things and many times in which you will have no control and all you can do is support and love. You will have to make peace with this role. It is not an easy role to accept. Before signing up, you should ask yourself if you are truly capable of doing this. If you are anything like me, a type A – boss ass bitch who wants to fix everything all the time, it can be a quite humbling experience. Opposite of a bio mom, a stepmother is choosing to be in the children's lives. So, if you are going to be miserable and resentful, you are not likely to give your best self to your relationship or the children. And yes, it is *definitely* possible to resent a stepchild and no, it does not necessarily mean you are a horrible person! When you enter into a new relationship with a single dad as a child-less woman, it is easy to feel jealous of his love for his children. You will want alone time with your new boo, date nights, day outings, Netflix and chill. However, he may not see anything wrong with constantly inviting his children. Nor may he understand the need to have designated bonding time for each of his different relationships. This can lead a person to feeling a bit resentful. Not only does this man share children and the child birthing experience with another woman, he also shares an incredible love for his children with another woman, who isn't you. He is constantly thinking about his children and prioritizing his time with them and you realize that you do not yet have a place at that table. Essentially, he is in full dad mode and you are the plus one. No matter how great your new man is at making you feel special and included in family movie night, family dinner night, family fun time, the feeling of inclusion and love does not just happen overnight. This existence takes time and effort to cultivate. Both you and your new boo will need to put in conscious energy to make this work. But, in the poetic words of mighty Beyonce, who wants that perfect love story anyway?

Being a kick ass support person does not mean you are not important or that you are settling. Being a stepmom does not mean you still can't be the princess or queen. It also does not define you as a complete person. Our identities are made up of so much more than just one role. We are stepmoms, we are working women, we are wives, we are lovers, we are warriors, we are daughters, the list is endless and unique to all of us. At any point during my journey if I was feeling lost or perhaps like I had "settled," I reflected and found that my issue was never actually with stepmomming. My issue was within myself and my relationship with my husband. Our balance was off, and we needed to recalibrate. I was supporting him, but he also had to support me. Your partner, as bio dad, must be willing to support you as both a teammate and life partner.

As women it is so easy for us to fall down the slippery slope of motherhood, we give our whole selves, and we almost always end up sacrificing our overall human happiness because of it. Of course, there are always exceptions. Like that woman whose only life dream was to be a mom. But to be honest, I am not sure I am convinced those women are all that happy. We've all had a dream job we aspired to during our childhood, only to get there and realize it wasn't as glamorous or romantic as we made it out to be… nevertheless, my point is, most of us have multiple layers to our identities. We need to feel some fulfillment in all or at least a few of these identities in order to feel true happiness. It is so easy to blame unhappiness solely on your role as a stepmom, because like I said before stepmomming is hard AF. Just as easy as it would be to blame your unhappiness on a dead end job or a shitty boss. But I have found that whenever I felt this engulfing feeling of unhappiness, it was not truly about being a stepmom, it was about my choices, actions, or my **lack** of choices and **lack** of actions.

Before marrying my husband, I had to ask myself if I was capable and willing to be a stepmom. Some women may scoff and claim that they always knew, as if they were born with a divine calling to stepmother. Some may think that asking yourself this question means you are not cut out for the stepmom life. Contrarily, I have seen those women jump into stepmomming without any active thoughts about it. Most likely looking forward to the ice cream dates and movies night with their new besties. Fuck that! I found that challenging myself with honest and uncomfortable questions has made me a better version of myself when it comes to stepmomming, wifing, and bio momming. For me, the most important question I had to address when contemplating marrying my husband was, "am I capable of balancing it all? Can I be a good role model for a child, caring for a child that will never truly "be mine," handling the emotions and sometimes drama from my stepdaughter's mother, be the bigger person, *and* maintain my own personal happiness?" I ultimately decided "yeah, totes, no big deal" … kidding. Actually, it was more like "Um… maybe? No? Yes? I *think* I can do this. This feels right." Despite my tenacity and resounding confidence – not – I was still completely unsure on what the future would hold. I knew that making a commitment of marriage to this man also meant making a commitment of love and guidance to his little girl. That isn't a decision I took lightly. I knew that my presence and my relationship could and likely would have a major impact on my boyfriend's daughter. I wanted to be sure and honest with myself. I knew that there would be tough times and I wanted to have an anchor to think back on, a time when I made a resolute promise to myself that I would be hundred percent in and would work through whatever came my way.

    I have met many women who have never asked themselves this simple question, "do I have the abilities *and willingness* to be a stepmom?" As women in love, we can easily get caught up in the proposal, the person we love, and be consumed by the short-term vision. Or perhaps we think that once we are married everything will magically change. I won't lie, part of me did think – or hoped – some things would change once my husband and I got married. Did I mention I was naïve? In fairness, some things did change once my husband and I got married. For instance, some of the third-party harassment calmed. My stepdaughter's mother did not immediately start accepting me as a stepmother to her child overnight, but there was a drastic decrease in the number of times my name came up during co-parenting disagreements. Although there has never been a verbal acceptance, there has been a gradual change in behavior over time. It has been a slow and minimal change, but a change nonetheless and this was a victory in comparison to what my husband and I had been living with. But I also know plenty of women who never share in this luxury and the treatment from the bio mom after marriage only gets worse as the new marriage sparks feelings of jealousy, regret, and a loss of control for bio mom. I say all this to make the point that, THIS IS A VERY IMPORTANT QUESTION. You should imagine your current life, in its current state, and ask yourself, "am I capable and willing to commit to this?" You should focus on vetting your partner. Does your partner support you? Does your partner put in an equal amount of energy into your relationship as you? Have you spoken to your partner about his expectations of your role in his child's life? Have you spoken to your partner about his expectations of your role in regards to his child's other bio parent? In my opinion, the biggest red flag is if your partner expects *you* to be the go between for him and his ex. This can go one of two ways. First, it could be amazing. You and ex-boo could become besties and co-parent your children as a big happy family! Or… it could single handedly cause you the greatest amount of stress in your life and set you on the track to an early heart attack. More often than not, it will be the latter. It takes a special woman to step up and be a stepmom. It also takes a special woman to accept a stepmom into her children's lives. Not all women are capable of this. Your partner should not expect you to be the primary communicator with his ex. If you and your stepchildren's bio mother end up hitting it off and forging a good relationship, that is fantastic! It should be organic. If your partner expects that you will take over the communications, it is most likely because he and his child's bio mom have not truly figured out how to co-parent. You can and should either A. Run away or B. Set boundaries. If you and your partner do not agree on this, you are likely setting yourself up for rough times or quite frankly, a living hell. It is *incredible* how much stress such a simple task can cause. Like trying to set up a pickup or drop off time with someone who truly does not want to be talking to you. I've been there. Avoid it.

    Early on in our relationship, my husband and his daughter's bio mom hit a point where they could no longer communicate in a healthy way. This put the responsibility on me to handle Facetime calls and arrangements. Despite the nearly three hundred miles in between us, I could feel the animosity as though it was in the room. I obsessively thought about and dreaded that seven p.m. five-minute Facetime call, all day. Despite all the struggles I have overcome in my life, all the adversity I have tackled, these were absolutely some of the most stressful days of my life. I overthought everything. Have you ever tried to get a young child to sit and talk on a video call? Young children are horrible about speaking on video calls. Should I facilitate a conversation? Will bio mom see that as disrespectful and invading her relationship with her daughter? Should I be in view of the camera or should I try to set my stepdaughter up in the corner somewhere? Should I bring her back if she walks away from the camera or do I just let it end? I also felt like we, *I*, owed these calls to bio mom, almost like owing a debt while conversely feeling like she did not deserve these calls. I felt like my husband and I would be beholden to a Facetime schedule for the rest of our lives and I hated it. I was beginning to feel like my life was not mine. I was no longer controlling my life all because I now had to be a mediator for my husband and a very unhappy bio mom. Thankfully, I do not remember ever having to say anything to my husband. I think he just recognized my anguish. This arrangement did not last long. Perhaps if I had approached that time in my life with the same thoughts and feelings I have today, then I may not have been so stressed. I was worrying too much about bio mom's feelings and not enough about mine or my stepdaughter's. At the time, I thought caring about bio mom was the right thing to do.

The Bedtime Drama

Why is bedtime always an issue? I have not met one stepmom yet who has not shared the bedtime battle. In fact, the bedtime drama is perhaps the epitome stepmom struggle. I honestly think there is no bigger or pettier an issue for a child and a strained co-parenting relationship than disagreements on bedtimes. People are just generally much more pleasant when they are not sleep deprived or spending hours every night trying to convince, persuade, even bribe a child to go to sleep. When children have two drastically different expectations of when and how to fall asleep at night, it can be traumatizing for everyone. Misery will most definitely ensue for children and parents. Seven long years in and we were *still* fighting the bedtime battle. There were tears, there are breakdowns, there were suddenly a million reasons why this little girl "just couldn't go to bed," i.e. bad dreams, hungry, sudden interest in philosophy and contemplation of the meaning of life. It also brought the "I wish I was with my mom" comments that are enough to drive any good stepmom absolutely fucking wild. I too would love to live a life with no rules or boundaries, void of general expectations to be a decent human being and provide for my family, but alas I am here "negotiating" bedtimes with a seven-year-old because I understand the long-term importance for my child's health, wellness, and development. What's the saying? "You-me-same-same, kid. Same, Same." Despite the constant overwhelming feeling to disengage, throw my hands up, pass the issue to my husband, and allow chaos to ensue, I chose to put on my big girl mom pants and give my child what I knew she needed to grow to be a successful adult. I CHOOSE to be her mom. Every bedtime argument, every vegetable argument. However, unlike bio momming, *none* of it is possible without the support from her father, my husband. If my husband did not support the structure and standing firm, it would be almost impossible to uphold order and provide our daughter with the structure, routine, and discipline she needs and is not likely to get outside of our house.

Early on in this journey, I would worry about almost everything when it came to my stepdaughter. Was she getting enough sleep when she was with her mom? Was she eating the right foods when she was with her mom? Are we doing enough to foster a strong relationship for her and my husband? The worries were seemingly endless. I had never been a mother before this. I had never had any exposure to a stepmother to know what was expected of a stepmom. I felt completely on my own and I allowed my emotions to rule and fuel my actions. As you could probably imagine, I was constantly stressed the fuck out. I thought nothing was ever good enough for my stepdaughter. I would always jump to worst case scenarios and feared the worst for her future. Would she grow up to be successful? What does she think as she watches this separation drama between her parents? As much as we tried to shelter her, I could see that she was taking on some of the stress. Somehow, my husband came to accept the situation much more quickly than I could. He invoked a plan that I could not appreciate at the time, but ultimately can now see just how magical it was and still is. He let go of everything he could not control, which included what happened while my stepdaughter was with her mother. That was her mother's time and the co-parent relationship was not yet one where he could have any influence. Instead, he told me that everything would end up fine if we only focused on *our* relationship with my bonus baby. I didn't believe him. He created a daily affirmation for our daughter and repeated it incessantly until she could recite it on her own. "*I am unique. I am strong mind, strong body, and strong heart. I am a triple threat.*" Even at the age of two and three years old, she knew her affirmation. We focused on teaching her to put herself first and everyone else second. We focused on building up her self-confidence and taught her about insulating herself from other people's anxieties and emotions. While I thought all of this was great to teach our daughter, I was not convinced that this would have any great material impact. Boy, I was wrong. Now, at the age of nine years old, my bonus baby takes responsibility better than most adults. She regulates her own responsible bedtimes whether she is with us or with bio mom. Of course, as any nine-year-old there are slip ups and challenges, but looking back, this focus was truly amazing. There is something to be said for worrying less, saying daily affirmations, and focusing only on what you can control. My stepdaughter, is in fact, turning out to be a strong and independent force of her own.

Joint Celebrations

Is there some unwritten rule that says to be a good stepmom, you have to *want* to participate in joint celebrations? If so, I would like to rewrite this rule right here, right now. Not wanting to do a joint birthday party with bio mom for your stepchild does not make you a bad stepmom. Nor does it make you a bad person. There are situations where joint celebrations work and there are situations where they do not. If you have a fairly good relationship with bio mom, limited conflict, and there is minimal risk of a four-hour birthday celebration erupting into harsh words or thrown drinks, then do you, sis. If bio mom is high conflict and brings you stress and anxiety, then why do it? Does it mean you are not thinking about your stepchild's happiness? No, no, it does not. Does it mean you are stooping to a low level? No, no, it does not. What it means is that you are taking control of your mental health and your house. You are prioritizing your wellbeing so that you can continue showing up as your best self for your stepchild and partner. Why does a stepmother have to sacrifice her mental health to be considered a *good* stepmom?

For my bonus baby's seventh birthday, we did our first 'joint' birthday party. Actually, it was less a joint party and more a party that we attended and to my surprise, put money down for. When it was all said and done, it went as well as I could have expected it to go. My stepdaughter was ecstatic when she saw her "Virginia family" standing in front of her in the trampoline park in New

Jersey. I received the biggest hug I think I may have ever gotten from my bonus baby and despite my bonus baby turning seven, clearly a big girl age, she spent most of the night running around with her toddler brothers, my bio children. Overall, the night felt like a huge bio dad andstepmom win and the happiness on all of my children's faces told me that we had done the right thing. It almost did not happen. Even though we had a couple of relatively calm years between us and bio mom, the reality of all of us being in the same vicinity for the first time since court was overwhelming. For weeks prior, my husband and I *stressed*. We fought about small and random things that we would normally never fight over. We both thought about it incessantly. We strategized and came up with game plans for all potential scenarios. What if bio mom was not happy to see us? Would a disagreement spark? Would her family intervene? Should we overkill the nice or just act cordially? How would our children feel about all of this?

The anxiety and anticipation grew. It did not help that we had a four-hour car ride to sit and stir on it. Not to mention that I had just entered my second trimester with my third child which made everything just that much more uncomfortable. In the end, we arrived at the trampoline park, found the birthday party, exchanged some cordial greetings and repeat introductions that none of us questioned, and then went our separate ways to stand by as our children furiously jumped around. It almost felt like we were starting a new chapter in our blended family relationship. It even felt great to introduce my young bio sons to their sister's mother and explain that is where their sister goes when she isn't home with us- a conversation I am sure we will revisit for better comprehension when my children get a little older. When it came time to do pizza and cake, we all gathered into a small room and happily watched the expression of joy brought to my stepdaughter's face by the presence of her whole family here, celebrating her, together. These are the moments that make it all worth it. These are the moments that teach me the most about being a stepmom, a bio mom, and a better version of myself. Unfortunately, many stepmoms never get to experience these moments, many times due to factors outside of their control. Let's normalize not judging a woman for protecting her sanity and potentially mitigating explosive situations before they ever have a chance to transpire. As I and those around me continue to grow and evolve, I hope we are able to come together to celebrate other milestones in my bonus baby's life, but not at the sacrifice of anyone's safety.

The Happy Stepmom

I don't know who needs to hear this but, stop making excuses for everyone. Stop thinking that you have to *want* to do joint celebrations. Stop trying to control things that are out of your control. Stop holding yourself to unrealistic expectations. Oh, and stop listening to every bitch that has an opinion. There's many of them out there. Bitches and opinions! Find something that works for you, in your heart and keep everyone else out.

For the first five years of my stepmom journey, I put everyone ahead of me. I considered the emotional needs of my stepdaughter, my husband, and even my stepdaughter's bio mom. I found myself making excuses for bio mom's immature and even hostile behavior. I would tell myself and my husband, "well as a mom, it must be tough feeling like you have to share your kid…" and "well, maybe she is just under a lot of stress right now…" or "maybe she is suffering from ongoing postpartum depression." In reality, sure, perhaps all of these are or could have been true. And sure, part of me did want to empathize with her. However, all it did was invalidate my husband's feelings and even more so, brought additional stress into my life. By excusing her behavior, I was setting a tone that her behavior was acceptable behavior, her feelings as a mom trumped my husband's feelings as a dad, and I was setting the tone that *my* feelings just straight up did not matter. While my feelings may not have mattered to a judge during custody hearings, as a motherly figure to my stepdaughter, as a female role model married to her father, my feelings definitely mattered. What I was doing was excusing the behavior of grown ass adults, as if they themselves were children. And this is not to say that I would expect bio mom to give a flying fuck about me, but as a mother, sometimes you need to put aside your emotions to act in the best interest of your child. This is true as both stepmoms and bio moms. It is not always the easiest thing to do, but that is a completely different conversation within itself.

Meanwhile, the real damage was happening in my relationship with my husband. For the five years, during which I was making irrational excuses for everyone, I was creating the perception that I was a crutch, taking on more and more emotional baggage. My husband was so caught up in the custody drama with his ex, happening on his left, that he hardly ever turned to his right to see what was happening with me. I was drowning under a sea of "emotional support" for my husband and my bonus baby as he was pouring more and more water on. It was as if he and I were out to sea in a sail boat during a hurricane. He was calling the shots while I sat by being tossed around by the waves. By doing this, I was also setting the expectation that I would never have buy in on what was going on. I would forever be the silent, behind the scenes partner. It made me feel like a spectator, as though I did not belong in this relationship or this house. In fact, I didn't really feel like I was part of a real relationship. My needs didn't seem to matter. My thoughts and opinions on what were best for my bonus baby didn't really seem to matter. I got to a place where doing things for myself seemed "selfish" while the other half of my family was going through so much drama and hardship. And the few times I did feel compelled to speak up, I quickly became "the problem." My husband had grown accustomed to my silence and being one less person to try to please, that when I made any kind of noise of discontent, suddenly I was the problem. Isn't that funny? I mean, not really... I had been doing so much to hold things together, but the moment I said something displeasing, none of it mattered. I had set the reality that it should all be expected.

I truly started to find my happiness once I learned to take accountability to hold others accountable for their actions and particularly their shitty behavior. Please re-read that sentence and let it sink in. I began holding myself accountable to hold others accountable. I was not just simply holding *others* accountable, but instead, my focus was on myself and my own actions. It was something over which I actually had control and I was taking conscious action. I realized that I could not control bio mom, or my husband, or anyone else. What I could do was ensure that whenever drama started to spring up, I focused on my own reaction. Instead of internalizing or blaming myself, I consciously thought about the issue and who genuinely was responsible. I quickly saw that very seldom was it me. Most of the time the drama stemmed from hurt feelings and insecurities between bio parents. I had to create boundaries. I devised a three-bucket plan in which to bin the drama. In the first bucket falls issues and conversation that I *want* to be involved in. In the second bucket falls issues and conversations that I *need* to be involved in. In the third bucket falls issues and conversations that I absolutely do *not* want to be involved in. Once I began structuring my buckets, I quickly found that most things fell into the third bucket. For instance, bickering between bio mom and bio dad equals third bucket. There is really no value I can add to this situation. I would not be able to stop the bickering and getting involved would only add unnecessary stress to my life. Thankfully, my husband also agreed with the "no bickering" boundary and also stopped engaging in unnecessary arguments with bio mom. Because, quite plainly, why? It brings absolutely nothing positive to anyone's life. Parenting decisions between bio mom and bio dad equals third bucket. It is not that I do not care about the decisions being made for my stepdaughter. At the end of the day, my stepdaughter has both of her parents here to make decisions for her. Adding a third opinion only muddies things up even more. In the past, I had been actively involved in parenting decisions, talking things over with my husband who already felt he was not able to truly voice his opinion with bio-mom. Whenever a decision was made that I disagreed with, I would spend days and nights worrying and stressing. Ultimately, I had no real power or say over the decisions that were being made. Despite all the money I spent on buying my stepdaughter clothes to bring to her mom's house, on child support, on health care, childcare, medications, I still had no real authority in the well-being of my stepdaughter. It was frustrating to care so much about something or someone that you cannot and will not ever be able to truly impact or help. So, I stopped. I needed to preserve my own mental health and shift my focus to making sure my stepdaughter had a happy life while she was with us. I continue to provide for her when and where I can. I just no longer have the expectation that it will be recognized or rewarded with decision making authorities. I now do it simply because I love her and I want her to be happy. Visitation scheduling for me equals second bucket. I don't get involved in the negotiations and conversations that take place around visitations and scheduling parenting time, but I do expect to be consulted prior to decisions being made. My family and I live three and a half hours away from bio mom and my stepdaughter. My husband does *all* the transportation- yes, our vehicles have truly seen some wear and tear. With three other children and my full-time work, scheduling takes a lot of coordination in our house. With such a long drive, my husband can be gone all day or even overnight to pick-up and drop off our daughter. Prior discussions on this matter are a necessity for me; basically, if it's going to impact the rest of our family, then I expect that my husband and I would discuss it before decisions are made. Otherwise, I try to bucket things based on their impact on my physical or mental health and how much positive value I can really add.

As a stepmom, we are expected to allow others to take advantage of us. Coming into stepmomming I willingly allowed others to walk all over me. It felt like being a servant in a rich man's house where you don't want to break anything, don't want to rustle any feathers, and hope to just blend into the scenery otherwise risk being chastised for poor dusting. It is a really strange dichotomy. While stepfathers receive praise for stepping up and parenting another man's child, stepmothers are expected to be selfless and open to abuse. It's disheartening that most of this poor treatment comes from other women. I often wonder why we cannot support one another and find love in a tough situation? Nevertheless, with a mix of personal accountability, creating boundaries that align with the three buckets, and holding others equally accountable, it really does not have to be that way. At least, I don't think so. When faced with a brewing situation, take a moment to ask yourself, do I add positive value to this situation? Does this add positive value to my life? Then ask, who is truly responsible here? If your answers are no, no, and "someone other than me," then move the fuck on. This one isn't for you, sis. It is not worth your emotional or physical energy. If you need to, explain to your partner why you do not see the need to get involved. A good partner will support your emotional and mental health, allowing you to inch away from whatever situation is threatening your stability. This way, when a time comes that your partner actually needs your support, you will be charged and able to help. There will inevitably be times that you will need to be involved or provide support. Those occasions are draining enough, why unnecessarily add stress and heartache to yourself when you could be preserving your energy? Afterall, one of you needs to stay sane if you want everyone to make it out of this parenting thing alive! Before both you and your partner hit your breaking points, come up with a plan on how to support one. Be proactive. Don't wait until you both burn out.

Holding people accountable does not necessarily mean confrontation or arguments. It can be reflected in the boundaries you set up and in your own actions and responses to drama or negative behavior. The next time bio mom changes the visitation schedule at the last minute or makes a crazy accusation against your character, just simply don't engage. Getting worked up and engaging in the drama tells her that she has accomplished what was likely her intended goal of either pissing you off or demonstrating her control over your life. Simply detach from the drama, choose to be happy. Minus some crazy outliers where bio mom is directly attacking you in a court document, then the drama is for your partner to work through with his child's mother. If your partner also sets up the necessary boundaries and disengages on all things drama, eventually the drama itself will fade. Bio mom will likely lose interest after realizing her behavior has no effect. Although this advice sounds so simple, it is by far one of the most challenging things I have ever done in my life. It was difficult to see my husband struggling emotionally. It was difficult to witness the effects on my stepdaughter. I wanted to jump in and fix it. It will never be EASY, but with consistency in your behavior and your actions, it will always get better.

I have seen and heard so many women try to rationalize or

excuse the behavior of their stepchild's bio mother. Like I said, I've done it myself. I often think that part of what makes me a good stepmom is my ability to empathize. These excuses may have made me feel better in the moment, but I was inadvertently creating a pattern of acceptance for behavior that I did not like. While my husband and I were still dating and working through custody agreements with my stepdaughter's bio mom, there came a point where I decided I had to step away for my own mental health. I had finally realized that everyone I had been making excuses for, were (surprisingly) all adults! Adults capable of critical thought and capable of demonstrating equal empathy for me, as I was giving them. The difference was, they were CHOOSING not to utilize those abilities when it came to me. As emotionally distraught and stressed as my husband was, the hard reality was that my presence wasn't adding any real reprieve. For my husband, I was just another puzzle piece to try to fit in while fighting to spend time with his daughter and trying to cope with his shambled co-parenting dynamic. For me, I was unhappy being second... or third... or fourth place in the list of his priorities. I made the tough decision that the best thing I could do for both of us, was to step away. He needed space to straighten out his thoughts, emotions, and try to build some type of healthy co-parenting relationship with his daughter's mom.

It didn't take long before my husband straightened his head out and came back almost a completely different man. A man more confident in his decision making, more committed, and more of a partner to me. As hard as it was to decide to walk away from my now husband and daughter, I knew that I was not happy and if I was not happy, I could not give my best self to anyone. I did not want to be just another stressed out presence in my bonus baby's life. Nor did I want to be a barrier between her and her father. I thought that if I could not be a strong, stable, and confident female example in her life, then I would be choosing to be adding to the dysfunction in which she was already living. I also knew that despite the love I had for my now husband, I could not be happy with a life in which I was constantly coming in second or third place. Some couples believe the children come first. Whether they are biological, step, adopted, or otherwise, the children come before your relationship. I challenge this concept. Children are constantly testing boundaries, learning new things and pushing buttons. They have daily mood swings equal to a woman in active labor, if not more. I believe they need solid and stable adults who can provide the status quo support that they need in order to learn how to calibrate their own emotions, how to interact in relationships both within and outside of their immediate family, and to learn right from wrong. My husband and I invest in our relationship first so that we can provide these things to our children. We can approach issues and meltdowns both calmly and strategically, on most days. Our children witness us working through our own disagreements, investing our time and reaffirming our commitment to one another and our family. They also see us loving one another and supporting one another. My hope is that they see how valuable a relationship with another human being can really be. I hope they can learn how to value others while also valuing themselves. As a mother, I can get *really* caught up in my children. Sometimes I need a nudge to remember this doesn't do my children, myself, or our family any favors. Part of my identity is "mom," part is "stepmom," but there are also parts that are "wife," "woman," "human," "free spirit." When I let those basic and fundamental identities fall into the dark space behind "mom" and "stepmom," a little piece of me fades. I can easily forget who I am. I can easily walk past my husband without a word or a kiss. I can easily forget what innately brings me joy and happiness. To circle back around, when I am not happy, I cannot be that solid, stable, and confident presence for my children, particularly my stepdaughter. My stepdaughter who has had to learn to balance two households at a very young age. My stepdaughter who has had to learn to adapt to two different sets of rules and two different home environments. My stepdaughter who needs to know that she is loved and has a positive and loving female supporter in her stepmom. To me, it is so important that my husband and I invest in ourselves and our relationship first so that we can provide all these healthy and positive lessons to our children. Not to mention, there were times before we had our biological children that my stepdaughter was with her bio mom. My husband and I were left to ourselves. And now, even though I have biological children with my husband that I do actively parent and whom live with us every day, we will eventually have to let them fly and pursue their own lives and relationships... (so they tell me). When it is all said and done, it will be my husband and I, alone, sitting at the table reminiscing on these current days of bio mom drama, crazy toddlers, a pioneering older sister, and a new baby girl. Hopefully, this table will be at a seaside bar in a tropical paradise.

Stepmom to Bio Mom

Love Them Like Your Own

    I am both a stepmom and bio mom. It, however, did not start out that way. When I first met my now husband, I was in my twenties, newly single, and childless. I was in Washington, D.C., living my best life. I was progressing in my career, hitting the club every weekend with my girls, doing brunch on Sundays, and at the gym daily. I looked good, I felt good, I *was* good. I met my now husband at a bar in D.C. and we hit it off immediately. He was handsome, fit, and nicely dressed. We started talking and, well, here we are today! I could have never predicted at that time that we would be here today living in a beautiful, quiet, middle-class home with four amazing children and a rather large dog, named Ruby. In the matter of only a few years, we grew our family, grew ourselves, and really began our adult lives.

    I have always known that I wanted kids. As the middle child and oldest female growing up in my family, I was always the caretaker for my siblings. I was mini mom. During high school, I spent any free time I had after school, sports, and work, volunteering with children's programs. I have always loved kids, loved caring for others, loved making a difference, and I could not wait to have children and a family of my own. When I started dating my now husband and we began growing and evolving into a family, I wanted more and more to have children of my own. I find this is always a difficult topic for stepmoms to talk about openly and honestly. There is so much societal pressure to love your stepchildren "like your own," so the thought of verbally differentiating between a stepchild and a biological child is guilt inducing, shameful, and taboo. The truth is, I love my stepdaughter with all my heart. She made me a mommy first. She came into my life at the most perfectly imperfect time and will always be my "first" child, my first kindergartener, my first big kid, my first teenager, my first high school grad when the time comes… but as a stepmom, I will always have to accept that I am third place in her life. As difficult as the journey to acceptance of this fact has been, I am now at peace with it. It is how it should be. My stepdaughter is blessed enough to have a bio mother and a bio father both actively in her life. She and I will always have a special stepmom to stepdaughter, bonus baby to bonus momma, bond. I have been in my stepdaughter's life since she was only a year old. Just like a bio mom, I have sung her to sleep, consoled her when she has cried, fixed boo boos, cheered her on, listened to her feelings, held her through sickness and sleepless nights. I have and continue to give so much of myself to my stepdaughter knowing that I will always be second place to her mother and even more so, third place to her mother and father. Now, I know there are exceptions to this. There are stepmommas out there with sole custody of their stepchildren after a separation from the children's father. There are stepmommas who have stepped in after the death of a bio mom or a bio mom who chooses not to be involved. To me, these stepmoms are all amazing women who have stepped into a whole new realm of motherhood with their resiliently strong children who, together, persevere. I simply cannot imagine all the experiences and emotions of these children or their courageous stepmoms. This is why I say my stepdaughter is blessed to have two bio parents actively involved. This is why I say I am at peace with my role as stepmom. As a stepmom, I want what is best for my stepdaughter and what is best is that she has two involved bio parents and an amazing extended team of supportive stepparents. So, when I say my "stepdaughter" or my "bonus baby" versus just saying "my daughter" it is out of respect for the dynamic we have going on in our family and for the positivity of my stepdaughter's situation. It is *not* because I do not love her, it is *not* because I do not feel she is mine, and it is certainly *not* to alienate her from her siblings, my biological children. It is to show her that I see her, I acknowledge her situation, I acknowledge our situation, and nevertheless my love for her remains unconditional as a mother to her child.

Over the last eight and a half years, I have seen just how smart children are. I began noticing that at the age of just seven my bonus baby was completely aware of our family dynamic. As I was pregnant with my second and third children, she and I talked a great deal about babies and how mommies and daddies and families are formed. She had a great interest in understanding why her parental situation was different from her siblings and other kids she knew. Interestingly, "decided" was the word she chose to use when asking these questions. She wanted to know how "mommies and daddies are decided." I suppose in her mind she was trying to make sense of the reasons why her siblings have a different bio mom than she and just exactly who decided this would be the case. She understood that I did not carry her in my tummy the same way I have carried her siblings. She understood that her bio mom carried her in *her* tummy. At an even earlier age, my stepdaughter was able to articulate who is her mommy, who is her daddy, and who is her stepmommy. Kids are so much smarter than we often give them credit for. I think so many of the disagreements and early stages of unwillingness to co-parent from her bio mom were largely based around the fear of not knowing if my stepdaughter would be confused on which one of her mommies is her bio mommy. Looking back, I can totally empathize with that fear. If only bio mom and bio dad could have talked through these feelings openly and honestly. We could have maybe avoided *years* of drama and legal fees.

For women who tell stepmoms to love your step kids "like your own," WHAT THE FUCK DOES THAT EVEN MEAN? This is such a loaded statement for any stepmom whether they agree or disagree. Let's unpack. Not all mothers love their children the same. There is no one way to love a child. I guess if it means that we should accept our stepchildren for who they are, even when they mess up… sure. If it means we should help with their schoolwork, kiss their tears when they cry, and love them for who they are as beautiful lights of energy… then also sure. But for the critics who see a struggling woman, exhausted from the drama and general challenges of stepmomming, and are quick to tell her she should not be a stepmom if she "can't love them like her own," I would like to remind them that there is a fundamental difference between a stepmom and bio mom. A stepmom wakes up every morning and makes a choice to be a part of their stepchild's life. Why do we all look past this as if it is a non-trivial task? If there is truly a such thing as love, to me, this is it. We CHOOSE to stay engaged and to care. We CHOOSE to fight and to parent. We CHOOSE to try, in hopes that our stepchildren will grow to be amazing human adults and that they will choose to love us in return. This love is a great love. It is also different than the love a bio mother has for a bio kid. Of course, no mother loves all her children the same. Step kids, bio kids, adopted kids, no matter who they are, each love is different. Love between a bio mom and each of her bio children is even different!

The love I have for each of my biological children is different. I love all of them equally, but differently. *Very differently.* When I was pregnant with my first bio son, I had an almost crippling fear that it would change my relationship with my stepdaughter or that somehow my love for my bio son would take away from the love that I had for my stepdaughter. Before you become a parent, it is difficult to imagine what the love for a child could feel like. Before you become a parent of multiple children, it is difficult to imagine your human heart being capable of expanding that love without exploding. So naturally, I feared that it would not be possible for me to love both my stepdaughter and my bio son equally. In fact, people told me that I wouldn't. Since the first moment I became a stepmom, I had people telling me that there was no way I could truly love my stepdaughter like a "real" mom. Most of the time I just shrugged these comments off. There was no way another person could understand my feelings for my bonus baby or husband or anyone at that. Nevertheless, the comments continued, and it began to sow doubt in my mind. *DID I truly love my stepchild? Maybe this isn't real love...* It is hard to know when you are a stepmom who does not have biological children because you do not actually have anything to compare it to. I started to believe the poison that maybe I did not *actually* love my stepchild. I tried to reassure myself that I did love my stepdaughter and that I was a positive presence in her life. I knew that when she wasn't with me, my heart ached. I constantly worried about her and her wellbeing even more so when she wasn't with me. And when she was with me, I wanted as much time with her as possible. I consoled her when she cried, and tried to make her laugh, fed her, dressed her, bought her whatever she needed and most definitely bought her a ton of stuff she didn't need. My husband would likely tell you it was and still is *too* much "stuff." Needless to say, to me, it felt like true love, but what did I know? I was letting people get in my head.

The most hurtful incident of doubt came about a year after meeting my bonus baby. My relationship with my now husband was moving in a positive direction, we were spending nearly every day together, sharing nights at one another's apartment, and I was caring for my stepdaughter at night while my husband worked as a bouncer. I felt I was putting my heart and soul into the relationship. I had completely given up my single, care-free life and was devoting everything to these two human beings. I cannot fully recall how we got onto the topic that ultimately spurred the hurtful words. My husband and I were most likely talking about a particular way he had handled a high conflict situation with his daughter's mother. These are situations I have since learned to place into bucket number three. While I may be frustrated by my partner's actions or lack of actions when dealing with our daughter's bio mom, I have learned that my after-action opinions only fuel both of our frustrations and disappointment. It brings about defensiveness, aggravation, and a sense of hopelessness. It most definitely does not add any positive value to the situation. The way I view it now, at year eight and half, verses how I viewed it then at year one or two, is that it doesn't really matter. I now understand that one action or inaction by my partner will not change much in our dynamic with our daughter's bio mom nor will it change anything legally substantial. And at the end of the day, I hold my partner accountable for his and subsequently "our" relationship with our daughter's bio mom. It is his responsibility to communicate with her and his responsibility to worry about it, so unsolicited advice from a third party tends not to be received as such a positive addition. It's like when you get into a disagreement with someone or a debate about a topic you're passionate about, but was completely unprepared for that spur-of-the-moment debate. Later on you think of all the great and amazing things you could have said to make your point. You imagine the glory you would have had if only you had thought of these things during the actual debate! Then you tell your friend about it and your friend has even more great content you could have used during that debate or argument. Eventually, you just become frustrated over the things you could have said, over the glory you could have had. What do they say? "Shoulda, woulda, coulda!" This was my after action advice. Yeah maybe I had some good ideas, but those ideas were useless after the fact. So perhaps this is what spurred my partner into saying the following hurtful words. Perhaps he was just not thinking when he said them, but hearing my partner say the words, hurt. It was as though my heart had been stabbed and all of my dedication and love had been overlooked or completely unnoticed when he said, "someday when you have kids, you will understand." As if I could not understand his love for this child for whom I had completely chosen to love and mother. I do not know if it was the look on my face or my completely depleted energy filling the room, but he seemingly knew the mistake he had made. Unfortunately, it was too late. To me, the simple fact that he thought I could not possibly understand his love or his "parental" logic, which for most of the early part of our relationship seemed to be more so fueled by the drama and emotions with his child's mother and therefore not very logical, told me where I stood in his mind. Despite all the progress we had been making in our relationship, despite the sleepless nights, despite my support and attendance to the endless family court appearances, he saw me in the least as a babysitter and at most a girlfriend who was "willing to help out." What he did not see me as, was a mother to his child.

I have since learned that perhaps this wasn't entirely true, and the real truth was that he was too caught up in his own stress and situation to really factor me in. Needless to say, a few months later for this and other self-preservation reasons, we chose to take a break from our relationship and re-evaluate what was going on. At the same time, my partner was also facing a difficult situation where he had to decide if he was going to temporarily house his daughter's mom in his apartment, after she had been kicked out of her parents' house. A decision I respected but could not say I accepted. In truth, he was in a no-win situation. If he had not shown her kindness and shelter, I likely would have judged him for a lack of fatherly duty and integrity. But on the flip side, I wasn't going to hang around while he lived with another woman. He was at a place where he had to figure out how he wanted to navigate his relationship with his child's mother, and I had to figure out if any of this was worth being with this man. Did I really need him in my life? Could I move on and be okay? The short answer was sure, I think I could have. I think as humans, we hurt, but pain and memories eventually fade. We eventually find new love and our lives go on. Luckily for my husband and I, the time apart helped us both to realize that we did want to be together and that going our separate ways would not bring either of us the lives we wanted. A few months later, having grown more sure of ourselves and of our relationship, we rekindled our relationship, he proposed to me in a helicopter over Niagara Falls, and I got pregnant with our first son. It was a happily ever after, except it was really only the beginning of our lives as a blended family and my life as a bonus momma.

When I became pregnant with my first bio child, I feared that I would learn that all this time, I had not actually been loving my stepdaughter. I was afraid that I would feel like a fraud. Someone who had been only pretending to play mother and love this child. Afterall, that is exactly what people had been telling me. I remember another day early on in my relationship with my husband. We had been dating long enough that I was meeting his mother, completely informally. We had been dating for at least a few months. I had been supporting my husband, standing by his side through court, and caring for his child. This was the first time I had seen his mother. She rather innocently thanked me for "helping" with my husband's child. Looking back, she meant well and was likely genuinely thankful that her son had someone on his side, helping him and his baby. But the sentiment that I was only here as "the help" and not a dedicated life partner who had been sacrificing my single life, stung and I was deeply offended. This idea that stepmomming is the equivalent of being a live-in babysitter or non-compensated au pair is one of the single most points of contention for women who see themselves fulfilling the stepmom role. Even more so, the notion that you must be married to the bio parent in order for society and others to dignify you even with the title of stepmom, is outdated. In terms of our dedication to our stepchildren, spoiler alert, nothing changes pre and post marriage! We do not suddenly change our behavior after the ring. If a woman is meant to be a stepmom, it is because she is a loving, caring, and compassionate person. She is likely already stepping up and momming well before the topic of marriage arises. In fact, this is probably part of the reason that a man decides to marry this woman! And what of those couples who simply do not believe in marriage. Does the lack of a ring make this woman less of a stepmom? Under US law, stepmothers have very few, if any, legal rights to their stepchildren whether they are married to the bio parent or not. My husband asked me once to make a doctor's appointment for my stepdaughter at a specialist. The slap in the face came when the receptionist would not give me an appointment because I am a stepparent and not a biological parent to my stepdaughter. It wasn't that she was preventing me from making a medical decision for my stepdaughter, which I could completely understand. Rather the insult was in that I was not even allowed to *schedule* a simple over the phone appointment, to which my husband would later take my stepdaughter. The real kicker is that my stepdaughter is covered under my health insurance, that I pay for… out of *my* paycheck! Once again, the double standards of stepparenting prevailed.

Surprisingly, birthing my first child did not bring about a profound revelation that I had not been loving my stepdaughter. If anything, it reaffirmed that I *had* been loving my stepdaughter and brought me greater confidence in my innate parenting abilities. It did absolutely teach me that a mother's love differs from child to child and a good woman, a good mom, gives each of her children exactly the love that they need, in the form that they need it. So, to all the bio-less stepmommas out there who are told that there is no possible way you could know true motherly love, you're not crazy, sis! Of course, you can and of course, you do. You are no less a mother than the woman who birthed those babies.

What did surprise me was all the emotions I experienced during my first pregnancy, and I'm not talking about pregnancy hormones. There is something different about going through your first pregnancy with a partner who has seemingly done it all before with another woman. I found myself wondering, comparing, envying, and feeling alone. To some degree, it really took some of the excitement out of the experience. I tried to grasp at things that would be a shared first experience for us. For instance, his first child was delivered by c-section. So, I tried to focus on the fact that he had never witnessed vaginal childbirth before or that we were having a boy and his first child was a girl. For some reason I could not explain, it was very important to me to try to find something we could share as our shared "first." I also found myself turning inward and almost walling my husband out of the experience altogether. I made it about me and *my* son, opposed to us and *our* son. My relationship with my husband had been strong at that time. I had never doubted him or his devotion to me in any way, but now with my first pregnancy, I found myself somewhat resenting him from "stealing" this experience from me. In my logical brain I knew this was not true. It was not as though I hadn't been aware he shared a daughter with another woman and how his daughter had come into existence. I may not be a scientist, but I know basic biology. I just did not think I would care. I did not think it would be such a big deal… until it was. Until I was pregnant. So, to shelter myself from these feelings of resentment and disappointment, I focused the experience on my unborn baby and myself probably more so than I would have if my husband had not already been a father. I focused on the differences of my pregnancy versus my husband's first experience. Now, being three babies in, I look back on this and realize I was putting way too much emotion into something that did not matter. Each pregnancy experience *is* different. Each one is like the very first one. For men and for women. Pregnancies are like snowflakes. It may be a blizzard, but when you really look closely, no two snowflakes are the same. Pregnancy is guaranteed to be a blizzard, but the reasons and symptoms behind that blizzard will almost always be different. Life changes, our body changes, and how our minds and bodies react to pregnancy with all these external and internal changes can be so drastically different. I became pregnant with my second son when I was only four and a half months post-partum with my first son. Despite being so close together, those pregnancies could not have been more different. Also, life is not perfect. It's not meant to be. As girls we are groomed to grow up, marry a child-free man, and produce children. It is the dream we are taught to have. That everything will be perfect. Our man will be devoted to us and only us for all of time. Every Disney princess ever has been able to achieve her happy ending by finding a child-less and hopelessly devoted man. Though, what happened when these princesses became pregnant and had children? Do those sequels exist? If they do, they came out much too late for my childhood and at this point, I don't even want to know what idyllic falsehoods they are teaching to the next generation. The fact is, life is messy. It is NOT ideal. And if you are a woman who subscribes to the ideals of Disney, then stepmomming is most definitely not for you. Stepmomming and trying to blend a family is messy and complicated. In this instance, the man isn't going to "save" you. He is most likely still trying to figure it all out for himself. Nor is he likely to recognize your need for help because *you* are now the assumed caregivers for the home; so, if anything, *you* will be the one doing the saving. Stepmomming is emotional, taboo, one huge contradiction after another, and non-ideal. Unfortunately, even if you go into stepmomming knowing this, it can still be hard to accept at times. Like when pregnant. Oh, and despite all that you do, you will still be viewed as the "evil stepmom." So basically, being a stepmom is pretty fucked up and unfair at best and you are not likely to get all those quintessential, dream like moments we have all hoped for since we were girls. It takes a truly selfless woman to take on the role of stepmom. But, for those of us who are willing to ride the waves of stepmomming, there are some pretty amazing rewards too.

    Making the leap from stepmom to stepmom and bio mom taught me so many valuable lessons in life, patience, acceptance, inner strength. If I could give that girl, my younger self, one piece of advice, it would be to "Let. It. The. Fuck. Go." Enjoy all the joys of your first pregnancy, unapologetically. Don't take it personally when your partner makes the unforgiveable mistake of comparing your pregnancy to his ex's pregnancy, reminding you that this is not his first go around in the pregnancy rodeo. Remember that there are reasons your partner's previous relationship didn't work out. Accept that every relationship has fond memories even if the relationship did ultimately fail. You yourself have fond memories from past failed relationships, you just may not have the evidence of that relationship walking around. Also, accept that welcoming a new life into the world is exciting but also a bit stressful and your partner is likely just trying to find ways to calm his nerves by making this a familiar experience, something of which his brain can make sense. In the end, when you are forty weeks pregnant with your little bundle of joy, on the cusp of forty-one weeks, all you are going to truly care about is getting that growing creature inside of you, THE FUCK OUT! Once that is done, all you will truly care about is caring for that baby and providing him/her with the childhood they deserve. Your feelings from your pregnancy will eventually fade, if not immediately fade once you are holding that little one. Years later, you may recall the experience, but not likely the resentment. So, try your best to just let it go.

 I was lucky enough, or perhaps, chose wisely enough to marry a good-hearted man. A man who cares about me, values me, and truly and deeply loves me. I know this. I also know that he can "mess up" from time to time. Say the wrong thing, *not* say the right thing, or be oblivious to my emotional needs. But, when it really matters, he is there. He is adoring, caring, and understanding. Once we began growing our family, any resentment I held, dissipated. For a large part, he has been a stay-at-home dad. Working for himself, his schedule has always been more flexible than mine. He has taken the kids to client appointments when he had appointments outside of the house and at other times, he has even had clients come to the house so he can care for the kids while he worked. He has constantly balanced childcare and his work for most of our early days with our children while I had to report nine a.m. to five p.m. to an office. Yes, I have been lucky enough to find a man who has stepped up despite his own occasional confused feelings over our "reversed gender roles." Ever since we both independently made that post separation decision to come back together and pursue our relationship, we have always functioned as a team, supporting one another against any internal or external negative force. No doubt seeing this man care for our children has helped me forget any lingering feelings of doubt or disappointment I ever had during my first pregnancy. Our life is far from perfect. Our relationship is far from perfect. We have children who stress us out. We have a bio mom who stresses us out. We have expenses that stress us out. However, when it comes down to it, we always have one another's back. THIS is perhaps the most important factor to finding peace in the role of stepmom. I have learned during my times of extreme stress and unhappiness – please believe there have been some *stressful* times- it was never bio mom or the kids who were truly at fault. It was us. It was the times my husband and I were not on the same page. The times we allowed bio mom to seep into our relationship. It was the times when I cared far too much about bio mom and put way too much energy into her actions and behaviors. It was the times my husband let his boundaries slip and we found the actions and behaviors of a third person dictating our own or forcing reactions. If there is ever any doubt in the mind of a stepmom, the culprit most likely is not the kids or bio mom or life. It is her relationship. We cannot control other people. We cannot change the past. We cannot predict the future. All we can do is control how we act, perceive, and respond to the actions of others and we can and *should* expect our partners to value our feelings and perceptions over any third party.

Mother's Day

I could not write this book and not talk about Mother's Day. As a stepmom, Mother's Day is one of the single worst days of the year. For full time stepmoms and part time stepmoms, alike. If "you are not a real mom" was a day, it would be Mother's Day. Hell, it *is* Mother's Day. I don't know about you, but like most men, my husband does not put a lot of thought into celebrations or holiday occasions like Mother's Day. Like most men, he is equally as surprised to see the children's gifts on Christmas morning as the children. Occasionally, however, he will truly surprise me with a thoughtful or romantic gift that I did not see coming. So, when it comes down on him as his sole responsibility to produce a celebration, it can be hit or miss. For a day that is already filled with so many mixed emotions, any little disappointment can result in a perceived heart shattering admission of one's inconsequential existence. As stepmoms, we make leaps to terrible and heart wrenching conclusions based on people's actions or inactions on this day. Husband didn't get you a card from the kids that says, "Happy Mother's Day, we love that you are our mom"? Obviously, it can only mean that he doesn't see you as a real mother! Your stepchildren didn't greet you with a "Happy Mother's Day" when they came down from their rooms this morning? Obviously, they hate you! In reality, what is more likely to be true is that your husband waited until the night prior before realizing the following day was Mother's Day. Tired from work, and already in bed, he idiotically thought he would make it to the drug store in the morning to grab you a card, but of course he overslept. Your stepchildren are children, whom unless prompted by your husband, are not likely to put much thought into the day. Have you ever noticed that children only get hyped for things for which we create the hype? I once hyped up my bio son with a game of make-believe when he was getting fussy on a car ride. I excitedly told him that a T-Rex was chasing us and he had to outmaneuver him to get to our destination. He now associates our family truck with a T-Rex and we can no longer go anywhere in that truck without a T-Rex chasing us. He will also come around from time to time out of nowhere and tell us there is a T-Rex in the truck. This has been going on for years now. He can't seem to let it go and it brings him a new resurgence of joy every time. You know what he doesn't talk about, ever? Mother's Day.

Mother's Day is a difficult day for stepmoms. Some of us will have to watch as our children make Mother's Day treats for bio mom. Some of us will even have to help our children make Mother's Day treats for bio mom. Schools will send home handmade arts and crafts with elementary aged children to their bio mothers. I have yet to see a teacher offer students the opportunity or the idea to create two crafts, one for bio mom and one for stepmom. I am sure there are some teachers out there doing it, I just haven't experienced it yet. There's also awkward tension within our social circles on Mother's Day. Some of our friends, family, or even co-workers don't know how they should treat us on this day. Should they wish us a happy Mother's Day? Would it be weird? Is there a stepmother's day? While great moms do not need a day of appreciation, it is nice to be recognized from time to time. Momming is tough. Stepmomming is even harder. Stepmoms go all year servicing, providing, supporting, loving, transporting, giving all that they have to their children and very seldom do they receive outward affection in return. Mother's Day is the one day our children are reminded to show a little dash of gratitude to a woman who helps provide them comfort and happiness, if not the sole provider of their comfort and happiness. So, it truly sucks when no one reminds them to do it.

There just does happen to be a National Stepmother's Day, here in the United States. It is normally the Sunday following Mother's Day and is meant to celebrate the very unique bond between a stepmother and her stepchildren. Does anyone actually celebrate this day? Outside of a google search, I did not even know it existed. On one hand, I love that there is a day dedicated to the special role a stepmom plays in her child's life. On the other, can we truly not acknowledge that a stepmom *is* a mom, deserving of the same recognition as other mothers on Mother's Day? Does it truly take away from bio moms to share the day with stepmoms? Celebrating a stepmother on Mother's Day does not diminish the role of a bio mom, unless she has diminished herself. I also do not see or know of many bio moms allowing their children to go spend a special Stepmother's Day with their stepmoms, if it does not already fall during bio dad's parenting time. In which case, what is the purpose of the separate day? Perhaps this indicates a positive step in the direction of stepmother acceptance and appreciation in our society. In the absence of knowledge, I will choose positivity and assume good intentions. But for every stepmomma out there, waking up on Mother's Day and hoping for some love, pick up this book, turn to this page, and read, *"Happy Mother's Day, momma!"*

"You Knew What You Signed Up For"

Bullshit. Prior to becoming a stepmom, there is no way one can really understand what it means to be a stepmom. Stepmomming is hard. There is no manual for stepmomming. There is no singular way to be a successful stepmom. If there was, I would be writing it for you now. There is, however, a community of women out there that have decades of lessons learned from which we could all benefit, if only we could stop criticizing one another. There is no such thing as the perfect stepmom. That would be like saying there is a such thing as the perfect woman. Who defines what is perfect? Let us normalize that a woman who chooses to be a stepmom is enough. She is worthy of the love and respect from all of us. She is most certainly worthy of the love, respect, and support from her partner. She is not evil. She is not here to replace anyone or to compete. These women have selflessly chosen to fight every day, through anxiety, disappointment, joy, and all the highs and lows of stepmomming just to show their children that they, themselves, are worthy of love. Not all stepmother-to-stepchildren relationships are the same. Not all families are the same. A stepmother must find a balance that works for her and her family but is wise to always keep her own mental health at the forefront. Over time, these balances will shift. Life will change. Nothing is forever and everything is temporary. She should not be expected to sacrifice herself or her mental health for this role. A stepmother can only be as good as she is *allowed* to be. She must have the support of her partner, bio dad. He must be consistently creating and enforcing boundaries that will protect himself and his queen. Afterall, a woman who chooses to unconditionally love children she did not birth, *is* a queen and it is her partner's duty to uphold such treatment. Our children are always watching and always studying. They will respond accordingly to whatever treatment bio dad nonverbally displays and allows. In most cases, bio mom will also only go as far as bio dad allows. The idea that any woman knew what she was signing up for before she chose to marry a man with children, is toxic. That is like telling a new mom struggling with post-partum depression, "you wanted this" or "get over it" as opposed to getting her the help she needs. We simply would not do that. We wouldn't let our new moms struggle. Our whole post-partum medical system is designed to provide new moms and their babies support. As a new bio mom you are flooded with nurses, doctors, technicians, and consultants nearly around the clock and that's all before you even leave the hospital. Once you get home, you make appointments with your obstetrician who asks screening questions for post-partum depression. Even your baby's pediatrician will screen you for post-partum depression. Personally, when I became a new bio mom, my mother and mother-in-law both offered their assistance through the new baby phase in attempts to help alleviate some of the stress of adjustment and chores around the house. As a stepmom, I didn't get an adjustment period. No one asked if I needed help. No one offered help or guidance. No one even acknowledged the new role I was suddenly in. It was almost as if I was expected to just know how to do this. I promise you, I did not. Nothing could have prepared me for the thoughts, emotions, and work that goes into stepmomming. Nothing could have prepared me for the disagreements my husband and I would have, some serious and some silly. Nothing could have prepared me for those first few years in which I felt very alone and as though I was an outsider in my own home; afraid of bothering anyone, of saying or doing the wrong thing; afraid of offending my bonus baby's bio mom by mistakenly walking through a Facetime shot. Or of the horrible things that would be said about me. No, there is no way I could have known what I was signing up for. And there was no way my partner could have known or will ever truly know, either.

If you are having stress as a stepmom, the real source is likely your relationship. Either your partner is not doing their part to make you feel valued in your role as stepmother, wife, life partner or you are harboring thoughts that you have not communicated with your partner. Perhaps you keep these thoughts and feelings locked up out of fear for your partner's response or perhaps out of a burning feeling of shame and guilt. Letting these thoughts or feelings simmer will only bring them to a boil later on, at which point it will be difficult to sensitively articulate these concerns. If you and your partner are not at a place where you can provide one another with a safe space to communicate your feelings, then that could be the real issue. It is not easy. It takes work. My husband and I are not perfect, but we both make the effort to be better for one another every day… or at least when it matters. I often remember the age-old advice that a relationship is between two people. Not two people and their baby momma. Not two people and their parents. Not two people and their kids. Of course, the kids are involved when creating a blended family, and of course the kids matter, but without the foundation of the *two people* there would be nothing on which the kids can build. To hope for success, these two people need to learn how to value one another above all else. Neither of you can allow a third party to weigh into your relationship or bring undue stress. Relationships are challenging and take work within themselves. Blending a family on top of that is like a tightrope act. One misstep and you pray the net will catch you.

To find yourself some peace, truly evaluate your situation. Do you really *need* to be involved in *everything?* Do your stepchildren already have two available and active parents? Ask yourself, what do your stepchildren really need from you? Do you really need to step in as the disciplinary? Do you really need to be the safe space? Do you really need to be involved in the drama or do you want to be? Be honest with yourself on the reasons why you feel you need to be involved. Do these reasons bring positive value to your life or your stepchild's life? Is it that you truly *need* to be? Are you afraid of being left out? Are you jealous? I don't think I can name any greater originator of jealousy than loving a man who has had the experience of sharing a child with another woman. This shit is hard to admit to ourselves. It really wasn't until I was expecting my first child that I realized I had been struggling with this dynamic. Do not let jealousy rule over your logic. Over time, it all gets much easier. Keep your focus on the present, what you do have, and the relationship you share with your partner. And when you can, communicate with your partner about your feelings, no matter how unsure or silly you may feel. All of your feelings are valid. None of this is easy.

Some women feel the need to be overly involved because they don't agree with the parenting decisions being made by bio mom and bio dad. One of the most significant personal transitions in my stepmom journey happened once I accepted that this really was not a good enough excuse to open myself up to all the extra stress. Yes, it's an excuse. I imagine it is similar to how grandparents feel when they see their children making the same parenting mistakes they did. Or how most women feel when their mother-in-law wants to provide unwarranted advice. Personally, now, I often sit back and think to myself, "well, we'll see how *this* one plays out" rather than get worked up over something I cannot really control. Because if it's not affecting my home or taking money out of our collective pockets, then it is simply just not worth it. My husband will invite discussion on most things, in which case I will give my thoughts, while trying not to be too pushy about it. If he doesn't come seeking my counsel, then it signals to me that he either feels confident in his and/or bio mom's decision and is not likely to be swayed easily or he does not view this decision as very important. Unless it is a matter worth going to the mat for, then why? Why invite the drama in? Why not trust that bio dad is making the best decisions with the best intentions for his children? Why assume that your way is the right way? Even as a bio mom, I have had to learn that just because my husband makes different decisions for our children than I would make, it does not mean they are the wrong decisions. I have had to learn to put my ego aside, put my trust in him, and allow him to parent. Now, conversely, my husband cannot make unilateral decisions that may also impact me or our children in some way. For instance, do not expect that I will be driving anyone to six a.m. swim practice if we have not discussed it first…

We all *want* to love our stepchildren like our own. But even our own kids can drive us insane. Stepchildren are no different and often have more adult situations to navigate than our own bio kids. So, while you are frustrated and feeling lost, so are the kids. They are equally as confused on the situation. So many stepmothers react to their stepchildren's behavior out of frustration and emotion. Many bio moms do this too- trust me. But as a bio mom, my first instinct is to give my bio kids the benefit of the doubt, something that I seem hard wired to do with my bio kids but have to do more consciously with other children. It is so much easier to accept the flaws in your bio kids than other kids. Some of us may have a hard time seeing those flaws at all! Although it's no one fault, this is incredibly unfair to our stepchildren. Stepchildren are going through the struggles of navigating their own realities, which often entails bio parents that do not get along, do not live together, do not do family meals or events. The constant back and forth from mom's house to dad's house where they live by different rules and expectations is a lot on a kid no matter their age. Be kind. When frustrated, take a few moments to breathe. Even if your stepchild seems to be testing you, or targeting you, remember that they aren't yet mature beings. They don't truly understand what they are doing. I'm not saying you cannot be frustrated or have your feelings. Remember, it is a completely normal part of parenting to be frustrated or overwhelmed.

How Many Kids Do You Have?

As a bio mother or adoptive mother this is such an easy and straight forward question. It's not loaded at all. There is no one to consider or think about except you and your children. The question equals, "how many children did you grow and birth?" or "how many children do you *legally* have, in the eyes of the government?" As a stepmom, this question can induce a shit ton of stress hormones. Personally, I can quickly find myself going down the rabbit hole explaining "well three… er four…well you see, three bio kids and a bonus baby from my husband's previous relationship…" I don't know why I do this. It can get even worse depending on who is around. If my husband is present, I fear that he may interpret my answer the wrong way, no matter what number I answer. So, my answer often gets long-winded, awkward, and the inquisitive party is now victim to my oversharing. In reality, the person asking the question most likely never cared all that much about my child/parent situation. So why over think it? I can tell you why. Because I let other people get into my head and influence my reality. Let's dissect the possible answers and the logic for a moment, shall we? First, I think about all the people who say that stepmoms are not real moms and that it is disrespectful to a child's real bio mom to consider myself her mother. So, by that argument, I should not consider my stepdaughter into my child count. Then in the next instance, I think about all the people who say, "you should love your stepchild like your own," so by that argument, I should count my stepdaughter into my child count. Then I immediately wonder what my husband would think or want me to say, which is likely a simple "four" followed by a lecture in the importance of making everyone feel equal. Then, I quickly try to decipher which school of thought the person asking the question may be aligned to before giving my answer. If the curious party is male, I'll likely say "four." In my experience, men don't delineate between children or really care all that much. They don't have the biological opportunity to birth their own children, so all children come into their lives the same way, as already made strangers. To most men, it does not matter if you have birthed a child or not in order to consider that child as your own. Now, if the curious party is a childless female, I'll also likely say "four" for similar reasons that this woman has not been through the very traumatic event that is childbirth. I assume, they are less likely to have an opinion on the bio mother versus stepmother drama, unless they are the product of a blended family themselves, which makes me assume that they would likely appreciate the inclusion from the stepmom and would agree that I do, in fact, have four children. If the curious party is a female AND a bio mother, this is when it gets awkward. This woman has birthed children. She knows the pain and sacrifice that has come with pregnancy, labor, and childbirth. I almost feel it is disrespectful to her to claim four children when I have only birthed three. Maybe it's because of my own weird internal perception that what this woman is really asking me is "how many times did you endure the miracle of life? Oh, is that all? You couldn't do any more, huh?" versus simply "how many kids do you care for?" Why do I assume the accusatory truth behind this question? I honestly don't know. I think it is a PTSD thing from childbirth. My brain and very bruised ego wear childbirth like it's a badge of honor. When my heart knows there is so much more to being a mother than physical birth. SO much more. And physically birthing a child does not immediately make you a mother nor is it the only way to become a mother. Also, I make a TON of assumptions on all these demographics whenever this question arises. I assume men don't care when in fact, they may! I assume that a childless woman has never had a child or may also not care, when in fact, she could! Needless to say, I am still working on this one and that's okay. I have cut myself some slack to not be perfect just yet and I challenge myself in the future to simply answer "four" no matter how much anxiety or self-doubt it may give me. Because I think that is what it comes down to in those moments. It is self-doubt seeding into my brain. In those moments I'm really just calling into question my own self-worth. Am I worthy enough of motherhood? Do I do enough? Going forward, I am actively teaching myself to not give a fuck what the inquiring person may or may not be thinking. Their opinion really does not matter. It does not weigh on the relationship I share with my bonus baby, one way or another.

The one exception, and potentially awkward situation, is when this question is coming from a medical professional. It is important to understand the context of the question. Is this person asking for medical professional reasons or are they just making conversation? Going through my third pregnancy and birth, I heard this question quite often. Doctors, nurses, random hospital employees, and it was difficult to know when they were asking for medical reasons or when they were just being friendly and making conversation. So of course, I offered everyone my rehearsed long-winded answer while my husband stood idly by probably annoyed by my near verbatim recounting of my parental history. Ultimately, I need to chill.

Favoritism and Dad Guilt

No, it is not you. Yes, people are likely "playing favorites" with your children. It is not always who they like the most or least, but sometimes there are unconscious biases with bio parents and even grandparents or other extended family. Listen, blending two families together is hard. Having stepchildren and then bringing new life in the form of a newborn baby into the equation can pose a challenge for people to adjust. Blending "his" children and "her" children together can pose those same challenges, if not greater ones. It can all be similar to welcoming a second or third bio child into the world. You may be scared, nervous, or even regretful for changing the wonderful dynamic you already had with your first bio child. It takes time for you and your partner to adjust. It is no different when blending a family together.

For four glorious years, my stepdaughter had her dad and I all to herself. There were no siblings to compete with for our attention and when she was with us, it was all about her. For those weeks, we essentially put our lives on timeout to spend time with her. My husband would take time off of work, I would greatly reduce my hours, and we always tried to schedule something special to do whether it was some type of outing, educational experience, or just fun family time. When I finally got pregnant with our first son, I wondered how my stepdaughter would adjust to the sudden change. We tried to prepare her for the new sibling, and I think she mostly understood what was about to happen, but like any four-year-old, I am not sure she was able to truly grasp the changes that were to come, until our son finally arrived. For nine months, my husband and I hyped up the idea of being a "big sister." We tried to work up excitement for this new little brother and I think we successfully convinced our daughter that she already loved her new little brother, even before he entered the world. She was super excited to have a brother, a friend with whom she could play and laugh. We talked about all the great things she was going to need to teach him and all the help we would need from her to care for our new addition. When I finally went into labor, everyone was excited. That is, until our daughter arrived at the hospital to meet the new addition, her new little brother. The meeting was lackluster and perhaps even disappointing in the eyes of our four-year-old daughter. I think we may have missed telling her about the fact that for the first few weeks or months, babies cannot actually *do* anything. She clearly had not been expecting a tiny creature that spends his days crying, eating, and sleeping. For as much excitement we had built over the gestational nine months, our daughter almost immediately lost interest. Even so, after we got home from the hospital, things went as well as we could have hoped. The nine months of building anticipation and forced love truly paid off. Our daughter exhibited no signs of jealousy or concern and in fact just genuinely seemed to love her new little brother. She wanted to participate in diaper changes and feedings. She watched over him as he slept and swung in his baby swing. Surprisingly, sibling rivalry was not our issue and never has been with any of our children. The issues came subtly from the adults in the family. Although, that is a different topic entirely. One that already has plenty of books written about it.

While I was pregnant with our first son, I had a growing, perhaps irrational concern that my husband could never love our children as much as he loves his daughter. Part of this was my ignorance for the boundless possibilities of a parent's love for their children. With each child, a parent's heart expands and is never at risk of overcrowding. Another part of it was also just how devoted he was to his daughter. He was a great single dad. Unlike what I had seen other men do, he took pride in his role as a father. He took her to doctor's appointments, cared for her when she was sick, put his life on hold just to spend time with her, spent thousands in court fees fighting to spend time with her, spent most of his life thinking, planning, and talking about her. Even now, I truly do not think we spend as much time talking about our four children collectively as he spent talking about his daughter during those early years. Perhaps it was first child jitters or the unknown of what the future held for his relationship with his daughter as his relationship with her mom was taking on water. Nevertheless, it left me feeling as though *our* children would never have a fighting chance at his affection. I was nervous for them. I vowed to myself that I would love them enough for the both of us. Of course, I didn't need to. As I later found in my journey, things tend to work themselves out in time. Nothing stays the same. People find new status quos, in which to live their lives. Parents find new abilities to love. But it doesn't happen overnight.

When our first son was first born, I thought I caught notice of some subtle favoritism coming from my husband and his family. I confided in my friends about my perception that my husband was treating our son differently than my stepdaughter. I constantly teetered on the edge of resentment for the unfair treatment and self-shame for believing my husband would do something like this. I tried to convince myself that it wasn't true and that I was making it up. It made me feel crazy. Was this really happening? Was I the only one who could see it? Was it because my husband did not love our son or was this an issue of gender-centric love? It could very well be that my husband had to learn how to love a son, just as he had learned how to love a daughter. In a perfect world, everything would be fair and equal and unchanged. However, our generation struggles with the tradition of our parents and the new age of parenting. We know that gender should not dictate our parenting choices. For instance, unlike our parents, we *know* that our sons can play with dolls and our daughters can play with trucks with absolutely no negative impacts on their lives. Yet, as we drive forward on the cusp of change, some old habits die hard. Maybe *this* was the reason for my husband's perceivably favorite treatment of his daughter. Nevertheless, it seemed to me like a stark reflection of his feelings for our son and for me. It felt as though we may never be enough to earn his unconditional love.

As it turns out, my husband just needed time to adjust to the new addition and I needed to learn how to communicate these anxieties and perceptions to him in a meaningful and helpful way. He of course loves all his children and with arrival of each one, I could feel our own bond and partnership growing. Afterall, it is now four against two! We must stand strong in battle! It took time for the treatment of each of our children to "even out." Once we were able to talk about it, my husband was able to reflect upon his actions. As parents we will not always love all our kids the same, but we must create a reality for our children in which they are all loved equally. No one is replaced and all strengths and achievements are celebrated. Despite my stepdaughter loving her role as a big sister, my husband had to deal with his guilt of not providing a nuclear home for his daughter, the same he was providing for his son and other children. Sometimes, I can still see the light dim in his spirit from time to time when she is not with us. For good men, this will be a life-long journey of ebbs and flows. And that's okay. Nothing is constant, everything is temporary. The best I can do for my husband is love him through it.

I too had to reflect upon my own actions when it came to the kids. It is so easy to be overly protective and defensive for a child that you grew inside your uterus and pushed out through your vagina (or via c-section), after all, it took a lot of work and sacrifice to get that child out into the world! There is also something to be said about the sleep deprivation that can make a new mom a little crazy. I felt myself becoming a little short fused on people, including my stepdaughter when she got too close or handled her little brother too roughly. Kids never know their own strength and for such little beings, they can be strong as hell! I was also trying to overcompensate for my son, for the love that I didn't think he was getting from his father. I thought my stepdaughter had both of her parents and didn't need me too. I thought the right thing to do was to focus on my bio son. Before you think about it, let me tell you now, this was *not* the right thing to do! It essentially led to my husband pulling one way with his emotional energy, me pulling the opposite way, and the children just left confused. COMMUNICATE with your partner. The subject of kids can be touchy. When we first started having conversations, my husband was defensive, and I was always hurt. He did not want to hear hurtful accusations from his partner like "you don't love our son." Unsurprisingly, this was not a constructive way to approach this conversation. But over time, I learned how to respectfully voice these feelings, my husband learned how to listen without bias, and we learned how to work together to provide our children the best versions of ourselves. Or as close to our best as possible.

I have heard of so many stories from stepmommas who have

felt their partners are playing favorites with the step kids. Unfortunately, not all those stories end up as great as my own. Some men are unwilling to address emotions and biases when it comes to their kids. Some women are unable to patiently communicate the issues without accusation. Some couples are never able to pull together as a unit to fix issues that impact the family. Some men can experience dad guilt so severe, it can end a relationship. The key to making any of this work as a stepmom is having a strong and committed partner. If he isn't willing to engage in the conversation and the possibility that he *could* be acting in the wrong, he is putting his ego above his value for your relationship. Kids or no kids, this never ends well for a relationship. Partners need to find a way to communicate, no matter how hurt one's pride may be or how "crazy" the topic may be. I have an ex-boyfriend who in no way valued me or our relationship, however, he was the first ever partner I had who validated my feelings and told me my hurt feelings "weren't stupid." I ultimately learned that he did not want to actually *do* anything about my feelings but could at least validate that no matter how crazy I felt, my feelings mattered… to somebody… just not him.

Dad guilt is strong. It is capable of making a totally rational man act irrationally or even "play favorites." While I was thinking "he isn't being fair to our children," he was thinking "is this fair to my daughter." And ultimately, he had every right to question that. Was it fair to bring new children into our lives? What would this mean for vacations and family events? Would our shared bio children live different lives than their sister? I believe this all weighed heavily on my husband and while I too considered these things, I was also thinking about the family that *I* wanted. As stepmoms, we are not supposed to *want* our own things. We are supposed to be selfless and needless creatures that can sustain our lives by simply pleasing other people. To hear a stepmom say she actually wants something is often viewed negatively. People respond with things like, "but what about the kids?", "you should be thinking about the kids", "if that's how you feel, you shouldn't be a stepmom." There is so much damn judgment. As if a stepmom is a superhuman being who has transcended above human emotions and desires. Or perhaps that a stepmom is subhuman and not deserving of personal desires and goals. As a bio mom I still have personal desires and goals, however, there is no one questioning if I'm thinking about my children nor is there anyone calling me selfish. In fact, it is the exact opposite. As a bio mom people tell me how important it is to maintain a life outside of my kids, to have desires, plans, and life goals. They tell me things like "that is sooooo great", and "aw, good for you", and "it's so important to get out of the house." What makes me more deserving of these dreams as a bio mom than when I was only a stepmom? Just because a woman has dreams outside of her children or stepchildren, that does not make her a bad mom or a bad person. It makes her HUMAN! It does not mean she is not considering her children or that she does not care about their feelings. A woman in any role cannot be expected to sacrifice her overall happiness for her children so long as her desires are not malicious in any way. But why can't a stepmom want biological children? Why can't a stepmom want to be CEO? Why can't a stepmom start a business or have hobbies that give her some 'me' time?

Children Are Not Tiny Adults

Stop expecting your children to be anything other than children. Children can be mean, ungrateful, and borderline little psychopaths. Accept it. It is hard for children to conceptualize a world at which they are not the center. As a bio mom, I try hard to instill a sense of gratitude in my bio children. Overall, they are good kids, but I honestly just think that sometimes it's the luck of the draw. Other times, I like to attribute my activities, behaviors, and state of mind during my pregnancies for my bio children's personalities. I haven't found any real science to say whether or not this is factual, but I imagine to some extent it has to be. Everything that happens in our bodies during the time of our pregnancies gets passed to the growing fetus. Whether our bodies go through a response to stress or enjoyment, whether we consume healthy foods or junk foods, I cannot see how this would not impact the baby's demeanor, likes, or personality. Nevertheless, it is hard to say what long lasting impact these things can have on a person throughout their life. It is also a lot easier to criticize someone else's children versus our own. How many of us have ever been out and witnessed a child having a breakdown or acting unruly? How many of us immediately had thoughts or even verbalized comments to friends on what that kid "needs" or what the parents should or should not be doing? Could we be any more obnoxious? I know that prior to having my bio kids, I most definitely did this. Once I had my own bio kids and experienced those completely random and unwarranted breakdowns in Target, I thought back and asked myself why instead of criticizing that parent, did I not offer help or a comment of support? Something to let that parent know that it was okay. Why did I think I was special, and I would never one day be in that situation? Honestly, it is laughable. I do not care how great of a parent you are, one day you *will* be that mortified parent in Target frantically trying to calm down your overly stimulated and highly emotional toddler. But, guess what. You will move on with your life. You will bring your child home, maybe put them down for a nap, maybe bribe them into tranquility with some mac and cheese. No matter what you do, all will be forgotten in a matter of a few hours. So then why do we expect our stepchildren to be any different? Our stepchildren are dealing with all their child and adolescent emotions plus additional emotions and confusion caused by their split house-hold reality.

I have been involved in many support groups in which some stepmoms are exhausted by their stepchild's behavior. They believe their children are undisciplined, disrespectful, and constantly acting out. This could certainly be true. We are currently facing a mental health epidemic among American youth. The Center for Disease Control and Prevention tells us that approximately 6.1 million American children have been diagnosed with Attention Deficit/Hyperactivity Disorder, 4.5 million American children have been diagnosed with a behavioral problem, 4.4 million American children have been diagnosed with anxiety, and 1.9 million American children have been diagnosed with depression. From what we see, the numbers continue to increase. With statistics like this, it is very possible that your child may be suffering from a mental health disorder, in which case I would implore you to seek professional guidance. It is also just possible that your stepchild is acting as a perfectly healthy, obnoxious child. Don't take it personally. Perhaps bio dad is not disciplining his children due to his dad guilt. Perhaps he does not want to be viewed negatively by his children or seen as the disciplinary household. Perhaps he just doesn't see it. Perhaps you are taking it all a little too personally. In fact, all of these realities could simultaneously be true! Children cannot always control their words and actions. They are impulsive and emotional. My oldest bio son will hit or kick his brother out of frustration over a toy and then come tell me that he hit or kicked his brother "on purpose." While I appreciate the honesty, he clearly isn't thinking rationally about any of his actions. Does that mean he's a bad kid? No. He just is not developmentally capable of thinking critically about his actions and allows his emotions to take control. He's frustrated, so he hits. He feels bad for hitting, so he confesses. On any given day, he will love a certain food and the next day he claims to hate it. These types of behaviors can be a lot more agitating when a kid that didn't come out of your womb is doing them. Remember to breathe. When your stepchild makes a remark about you or to you, remember that is not your child talking. That is more likely something that has been planted into your child. Or it is your child voicing their overly confused thoughts and emotions. Children are porous and absorb everything they see, hear, and feel around them. They are hearing the words that their adults say. They are adopting the feelings that their adults feel. They are also kids who are naturally going to test boundaries. Try your best to keep your head high, keep your cool, and do what you do best. Love. And let's cut each other some slack. Let's normalize a stepmom at her breaking point not being perfect. Let's practice forgiveness for one another and most importantly for ourselves. Afterall, we are also only human. We were once those young children trying to figure it out and testing boundaries. As a stepmom, I'm not sure much has changed. We are still trying to figure it out and testing the social boundaries we were raised to uphold.

Court

If there is something most stepmommas have in common, it is that we are self-taught legal advisors. We have researched family court law as though we were studying for the Bar exam. Most of us know our partner's custody agreement better than they do themselves and a hell of a lot better than bio mom, who oddly seems to have never read the agreement despite her lawyer having drafted most of it. Most stepmoms have been through the worst of the American family court system. A system that at times feels as though it has been designed to keep fathers away from their children and to keep children fatherless. I said what I said.

For five years I watched my husband do everything he was supposed to do while bio mom blew off court dates, made false accusations, breached temporary agreements, withheld our daughter, and just generally gave no fucks. We showed up for all eight a.m. court appointments three states away from our home state, we spent thousands on an attorney who was presumably well liked in the New Jersey family court circuit, my husband followed all court orders precisely. During one court appearance we straight up wrote a check to bio mom like some real New Jersey pay off shit. Despite doing all the things he was expected to do and then some, we still ended up with some real crap custody agreement. After so many years and so much drama, we were physically and emotionally exhausted. We wanted the fighting to end. Our lawyer told us that until our daughter turns a certain age, my husband most likely had no shot at getting physical custody in the New Jersey system as the system, more often than not, favored the mother. Of course, we had to go get a second opinion, which turned out to be almost identical to the first opinion. After accruing so much in legal debt and so many years of arguing, the best advice we received from our "prodigious" lawyer was "unless [bio mom] is caught committing a negligent act and your daughter is near death, this is as good as you are going to get. Just sign it." The agreement she was asking my husband to sign outlined bio mom having school time custody, bio mom and bio dad sharing most major holidays, forcing some logistical acrobatics on our and our daughter's part, and trading off every two weeks during the summer months. The burden of all logistics falling on us and our daughter. I was frustrated by this arrangement. To me, it seemed to only take into consideration bio mom, not bio dad and certainly not the child at the center of it all. Or perhaps it was a show that even our lawyers were just over it. Drained, defeated, and missing his daughter, my husband signed. As time has gone on, I think even bio mom has realized how little sense this agreement has actually made. It forces our young daughter to spend a lot of time traveling on the Rt 95 corridor during short spurts of time and only having short stays for bonding time with her dad and siblings. Thankfully, in our case, both bio mom and bio dad seem to be reconciling that an agreement made in the thick of raw emotion, may not have been the best agreement. Also, in a twist of events, a global pandemic and lock down forcing most children to stay home and learn virtually may have helped persuade bio mom that perhaps she needed some help. Despite all the negatives we faced with the COVID-19 pandemic, it brought us much more time with our daughter. It taught me to try looking for the positives in an otherwise not so positive situation.

I began believing that maybe, just maybe, there *is* a silver lining in everything.

I have spoken with so many stepmoms who have had all too similar court experiences across multiple states. The benefit of the doubt goes to bio mom while bio dad must prove he is worthy to spend time with his children. Perhaps if I ever find myself personally in the midst of a legal separation, I will be grateful for the latitude granted to me as bio mom. I would like to think that I would still see it for what it is. My hope is that in the future we can work toward changing the way our legal system sees child custody cases. These cases are not simply two adults arguing for control over property, much like a car or a house. These court officials are being entrusted to help two feuding, bruised ego, emotionally hurt adults compromise on the best possible scenario for the children caught in between a failed relationship. Whatever agreement comes out of the process most likely lays the groundwork for defining and shaping these children's lives, values, and personalities. The emphasis should be on the physical and emotional burdens of our children, not on the grown adults, despite how much they may act as though they are children.

The Petty Sh**

It would be a missed opportunity if we did not talk about some of the pettiness we experience as stepmoms. Although some of it is minor and we can laugh it off, some of it can cause real anxiety and hurt. High conflict bio mom trauma is most definitely a real thing that too many women are forced to put up with just to live their lives with their partners and stepchildren. Thankfully, through boundary setting and time and distance, my husband, bio mom, and I have put these days behind us… for now.

One of the pettiest things I think most stepmoms can relate to, is the fight over clothing. Hey, remember that one time bio mom sent her child to bio dad's house with a nice pair of pants and you, stepmom, accidentally lost track of them and instead sent the child back with an equally nice pair of pants but not *the* pair of pants and now bio mom will only send her child to you in clothing that is two sizes too small or not weather appropriate because "she'll never get it back?" Or remember that family picture you have posted on your social media page for your friends and family? The one that includes you *and* your bonus baby!? The one that you should take down because "you are not their mom?"

Remember the time you were accused of brainwashing your stepchild against their bio mom because, well, fill in the blank with the flavor of the week excuse. It seems whenever bio mom commits a parenting error or your stepchild is upset with their bio mom, it is the stepmother and bio dad's fault for brainwashing the children. Please stepmoms, stop with the voodoo.

Don't get it twisted, bio moms are not the only moms capable of pettiness. Sometimes a stepmom needs a good petty incident to keep her sanity. Sometimes she needs to rebuke pettiness with pettiness, though I would not recommend doing it all the time. It will only result in a continuous loop of frustration and petty bombs being dropped in the road for each of you to step over. It's basically how I feel when I play Mario Cart with the kids, "*another lap? What just exploded on me? Am I dead yet? Is this over?"* I am not a gamer, to say the least. I have known some stepmoms to do some equally petty shit, fortunately this is not a book about the petty shit stepmoms can do! What I will say about it, however, is that petty actions are often based in negative emotions. As petty as I want to be at times, I always try to take a step back and assess why I am feeling the way I am. Is it worth my time and energy? Will this bring me positive value? Will I feel good about myself when it is all said and done? Most of the time, it just isn't worth it. But if that's how you roll, then do you, sis!

The Burnout

Stepmoms can burn out too! Whether you have the kids on a full-time schedule or a part time schedule, stepmomming is exhausting. It is okay to feel down or tired or a little like throwing in the towel. Stepmoms are constantly in a state of "trying" that can really wear a woman down. Unlike bio moms, stepmoms are almost always trying to prove themselves to their stepchildren, their partners, and yes, even bio mom. Sometimes it can feel like you have to prove yourself to the world. It also can often feel like the littlest transgression or unfavorable request from a stepmom can escalate into a fissure in the household and threaten to tear apart her relationships. Stepmomming takes courage. Courage to be bold, to run your home unapologetically. Courage to navigate sensitive discussions with potentially nonreceptive partners. Courage to love with no promise of love returned. And in some instances, the actual courage to stand against potential threats from upset bio moms. And the women known as "stepmom" deal with all of this all while wearing a smile and trying to be the bigger person. Being courageous and strong ALL OF THE TIME can really burn a person out. Being the bigger person ninety-five percent of the time in most of our relationships can really take a person close to their boiling point. Let's be honest, sometimes the only thing giving us sanity is that five percent when our inner petty slips out before the logical brain has an opportunity to take the high road. Which is what we do. Stepmoms constantly take the high road in disagreements with bio parents, particularly with bio mom. When bio mom goes low, stepmom is forced to go high. And do you know what you will find on top of all the trying? Do you know what is waiting there to reward these women for all their courage and exhaustion? The boogie eating, attitude giving children! The children for whom we endure so much. The tweens sitting on the couch giving attitude about chores or the toddlers having a break down over something seemingly inconsequential. On those days where it all feels too much, when life is coming at you fast, it can be hard to remember why you signed up for such an impossible and ungrateful role. When your world is falling apart, laundry is building up, all your dishes somehow seem to be dirty, bio mom seems to have yet another problem with you mothering her children, your partner is consumed by work and unable to provide support, and your kids are going through one of their "moods", it can be difficult to find solace in any of it. It can be easy to throw your hands up or break down. Girl, do not hold it in! I have found that a good breakdown can be cleansing. Visualize each tear that falls as though it is washing away a little piece of the stress, anxiety, and thoughts of imperfection. Eventually you will look down and see all that self-doubt, frustration, and insecurity laying in a puddle on the floor, completely extinguished from your body. Let it out. Do not let those negative thoughts and feelings fester within you or consume you. You, stepmom, are a boss babe badass and even boss babe badasses need an outlet. There is nothing easy about momming. Being a mom is the most difficult of all my identities. And there are days that I just, quite frankly, do not feel like doing it. Yet as stepmoms we continue to pick ourselves up, brush ourselves off, and choose to be involved. We each find something to hang onto during times of extreme turmoil. We find something that stops us from walking or running away. For me, it is a bit of simple stubbornness. For one, I do not want to give others the satisfaction of my 'failure'. And more importantly, it is a feeling of destiny. As though I am exactly where I am meant to be. It is an overwhelming feeling that I was brought here with my bonus baby by fate. I believe that our relationship was, and still is, very special. Every stepmomma needs to find her grounding. Once you find it, hang onto it and don't forget to wear a seatbelt.

There is no shame in burning out. Even with a supportive partner, sweet children, and an amicably co-parenting bio mom, it is still possible to reach a burnout point. Even with positivity or a good stride, it is still possible to reach a burnout point. Having a moment where things are going well or smoothly does not mean that they do not take effort. Sometimes things are only going well because you have or are putting in effort, a LOT of effort, and that can be exhausting. It can feel like as a stepmom you are expected to hold it altogether. To be the peacemaker between all parties, to be the compassion when it is lacking, to be the voice of reason, the bigger person, the supportive partner, the loving mother, the calm through the chaos, the maid, the chef, and the provider. As much as you provide support to your partner, your partner must also remember to provide support to you. Your relationship should always be a two-way street with equal amounts of love and support going each way. If this is not happening, speak up. Let's normalize communicating our needs.

Stepmom Wins

Making It All "Worth It"

Being a stepmom has its challenges, but it also has some utterly amazing moments. While this book has been an opportunity for me to speak about the often-difficult and raw emotions behind stepmomming, it would be a blunder not to discuss the many wonders of stepmother-hood. For all the new stepmommas out there who may be reading this book or who may have joined that support group, not every day is doomsday! For all the experienced stepmommas out there, if every day *is* doomsday, I encourage you to re-evaluate your situation. It should not be that way. While so many of us share in the challenges, we also share the joy. Sometimes we just need to vent our feelings with an empathetic audience. This book is meant to do nothing more than to start that conversation. I hope we can begin normalizing the discourse and acceptance of human emotions for a population of women who are going above and beyond for our families every day. And, stepmommas, I hope we can start finding our happiness in the seemingly small and mundane tasks we do every day. The same trivial tasks that can often stress us out or overwhelm us are the same things that may make a world of difference to our children. Afterall, these are the things that mean the most to our children. These are the things that give our kids that feeling of comfort and security that will give them the strength and self-confidence they will need as they traverse through life. It is the warm and toasty "apple pie at

Thanksgiving" vibes that our children will one day share with their partners when reminiscing on their childhoods. You may not get that glowing "thank you" right now, but one day it will come. It may be a vocal "thank you" or it may be a silent "thank you"; a "thank you" that comes as a mother-son dance at your son's wedding or a request to be close by when your daughter gives birth to *her* first baby. Watch out for them, or you may miss them!

Most stepmoms can recount each time their children have expressed their love and appreciation for them. As a bio mom, I receive "I love you's" and shows of affection from my bio kids daily, sometimes by the minute. Sometimes when all I am trying to do is sleep, eat, work, or write a book, I cannot escape the shower of love. As a stepmom, it is not always the same. While I know my bonus baby shares in my love and appreciation, it is not always displayed the same way. So, far I have experienced three wonderful instances in which my daughter has shown her emotion toward me. Luckily, I was able to capture two with a photo. Just thinking about these moments fill me with love, bring tears to my eyes, and make it all "worth it." There, of course, have been other smaller moments that we have shared that I would most definitely consider as "stepmom wins", like when we showed up to my daughter's joint birthday party and I received the biggest run-into-a-hug I have ever received from my daughter. It was an unabandoned, unabashed, all out, happy-to-see-me, love filled hug as my family and bio mom's family all looked on. I felt a surge of love and pride. In moments like those, I am reminded why I choose to stepmom. They teach me not to take any moment for granted. They teach me how to appreciate the little things that our children show us. They teach me how to be a better stepmom and a better bio mom. Heck, they teach me how to be a better human. They remind me what matters most in this life; time with our families and cherishing every moment we have with our children, whether it is every-other-weekend, summer break, or primary physical custody. Being a stepmom is most *definitely* "worth it."

You're Not Crazy, Sis

As I sat to write this book, trying to decide which of my experiences to include and which of the most delicate topics to engage, I went through an array of emotions from apprehension to excitement. Apprehension for talking about something so personal and taboo. Excitement for finally getting my voice out there and starting a conversation. I could have given this book so many different titles, for instance *"Stepmomming: It's Not All Fun and Games," "Stepmomming: What the Fu**?", "Stepmomming: Proceed with Caution."* Ultimately, I found these titles to be misleading, although an accurate reflection of the realities at times. Stepmomming is not all doom and gloom. Much like being any parent, stepmomming has its highs and lows. There are so many joys that come from being a stepmom. There are the joys of watching your children grow up and learn new things. There are the joys of growing with your partner as a couple and as parents. There are the joys of family vacations, school accomplishments, those times you *do* get an "I love you" from your child, and all of the many stepmom wins even if they take years to come. This book is not to say that stepmomming is impossible or cannot or should not be done. This book is to say that this stepmomming thing is hard, but you are not alone. There are so many stereotypes, dynamics, drama, and headaches stepmoms must deal with that traditional moms simply do not. That does not mean a stepmom's trials and pain are abnormal. In fact, it's unfortunately all very normal. Until our society changes the way we view the roles of women and our ideals around our family structures, stepmomming will remain a challenge for many. Whenever you feel helpless or hopeless, know that there are hundreds of thousands, if not millions of women across the globe fighting these same struggles. We will continue to pioneer for the future. We will continue to love with all we have. We will continue to provide for our children. We will remain resilient, strong women. We will show our sons the power of a woman who chooses to show up. We will teach them how to respect a fierce woman. We will show our daughters the true spirit of a tenacious woman who will win through love and acceptance. We will force the conversations to continue so that our children can be cared for properly and grow with a sense of safety and comfort. Afterall, a child who feels safe, is more likely to try for success. And I hope we will begin to support one another.

As you go out into the world, I hope this book has left a little imprint. I hope you have those conversations with your partner, the ones you have been putting off out of trepidation. I hope you set and enforce boundaries that protect your mental health and happiness. I hope you command the respect that you deserve. I hope you evaluate your relationship with your partner and identify the areas that need development. I truly hope you receive the support you will need from your partner in order to be successful. Without the support of your partner, you are bound to have one hell of an experience. Stepmomming will not always be easy, but you were built tough. Sometimes all it takes is knowing that you are not alone. There will be times when others may want you to believe you are exaggerating, or that your feelings are not valid. They will want you to believe it's you, not them. You will go around in circles feeling crazy questioning yourself, *"is it me?"* Do not allow others to cause you to question yourself. Find your spirit, find your stepmom purpose, keep true to your integrity. Strong mind, strong body, strong heart. You are a triple threat. From one stepmom to another, keep doing you. You are not crazy, sis.

Final words from the author:

Thank you for sharing in my journey and allowing me to document all that makes me human while I learn how to be a stepmom. For all the stepmoms reading, I hope you can find some reflections of yourselves or your life experiences in my own stories. I think so much of what we experience as stepmothers is truly universal. These challenges cut across culture, across race, and across socio-economic statuses. We are women trying to be everything to everyone. Let's promise to support one another and show up with empathy and compassion. Our world may not yet recognize the challenges we face, but they never will if we do not speak about them. At a time when women are doing it all, going to space, cooking homemade meals, doing dance drop offs, and running companies, there should be nothing holding us back from speaking our truth.